These 50 images and extra blank spaces are for you to color, doodle, jot down your ideas, ANYTHING you want! Add your own special style and make these pages your own. Most importantly, have fun!

EVERY MOMENT

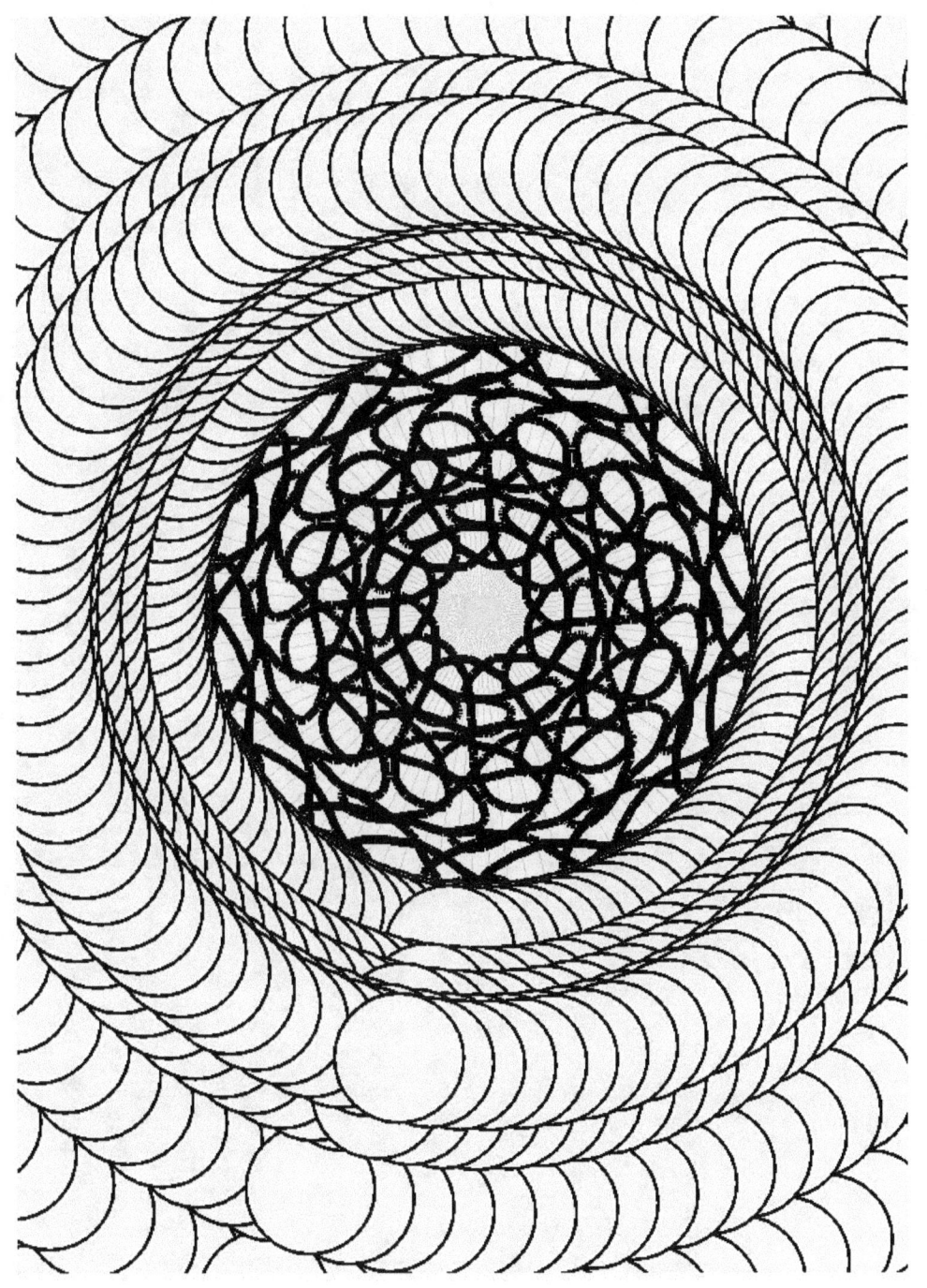

COUNTS

YOU ARE POWERFUL

BEYOND LIMITS

ANYTHING IS POSSIBLE

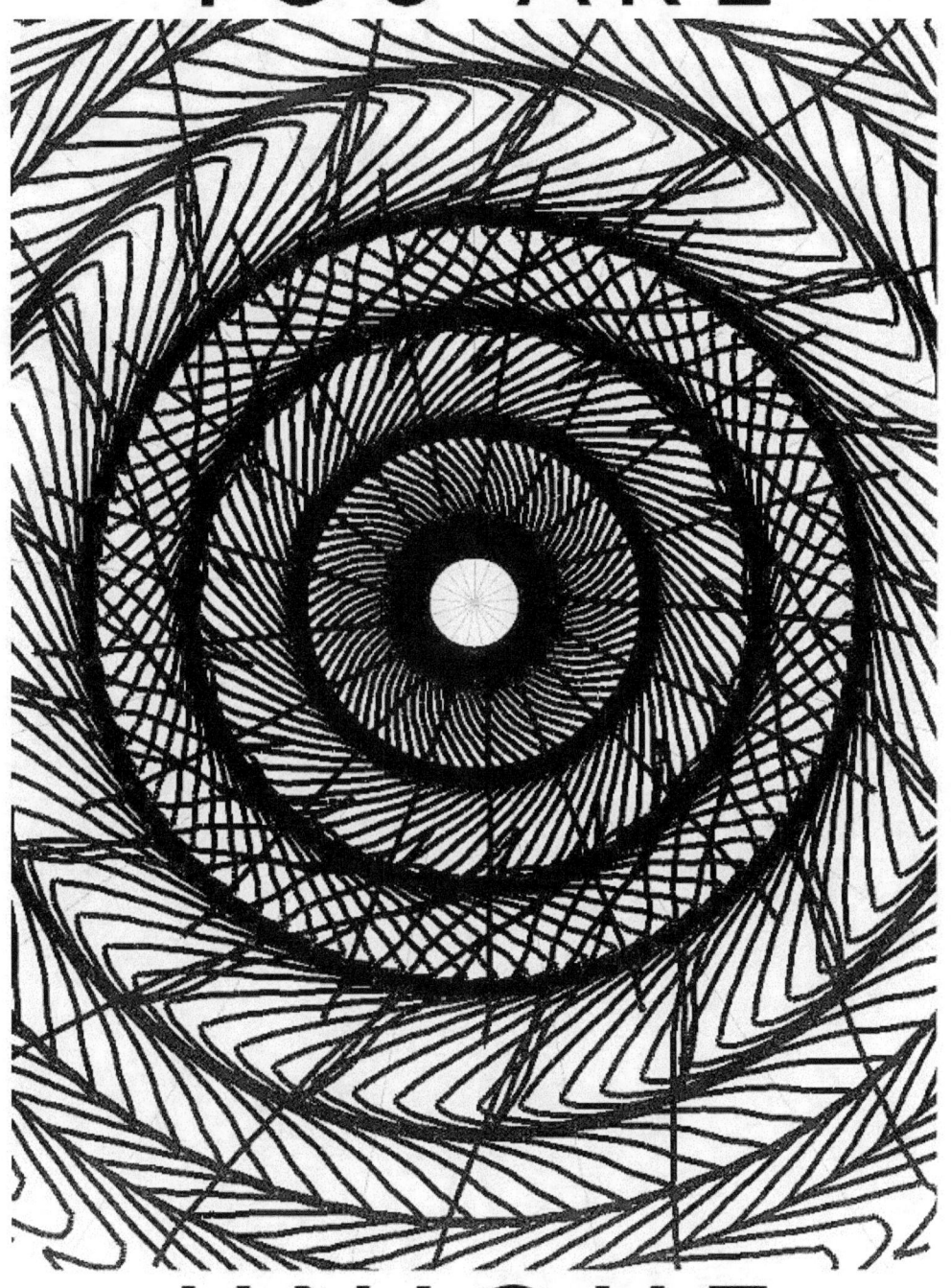

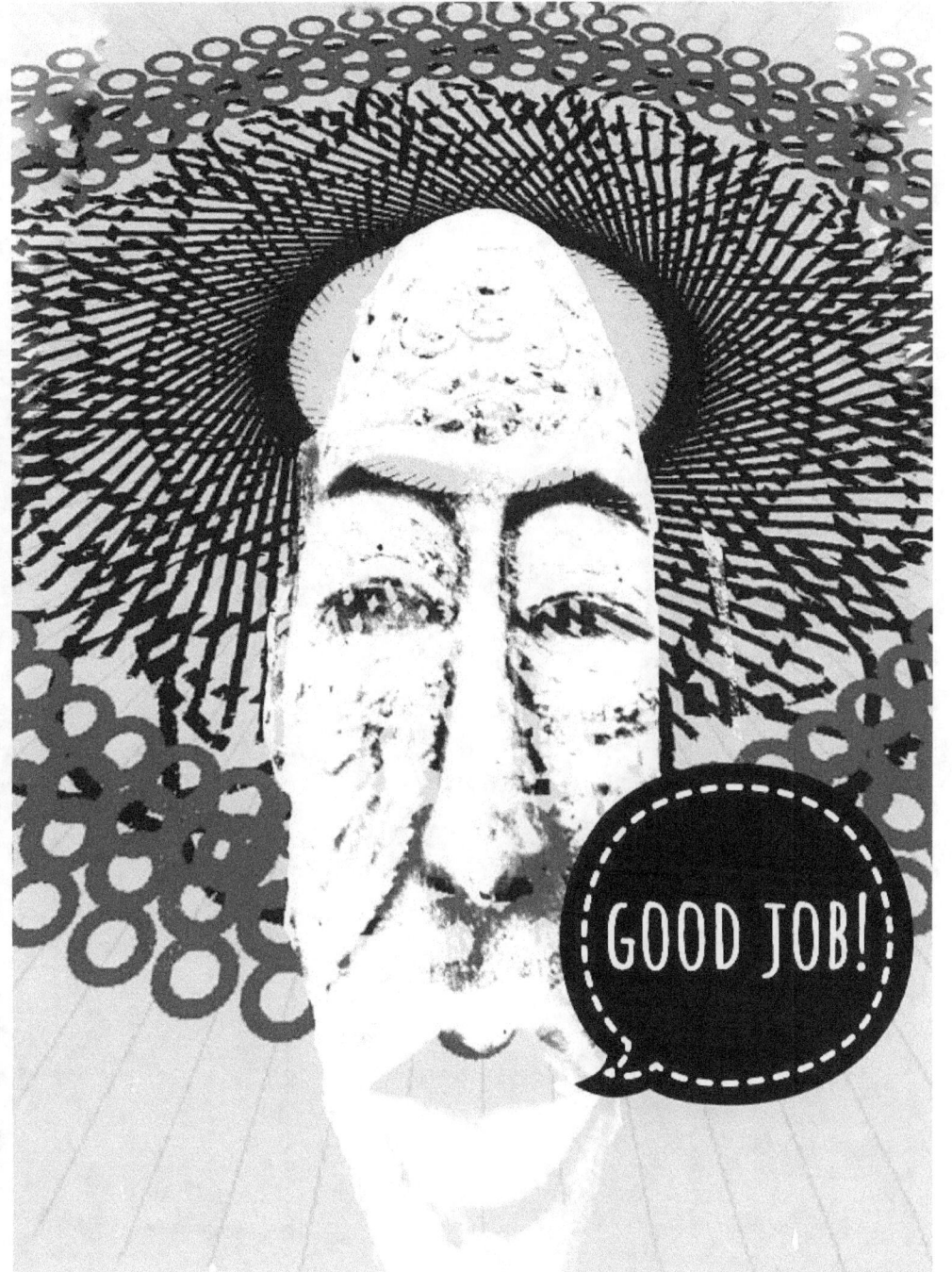

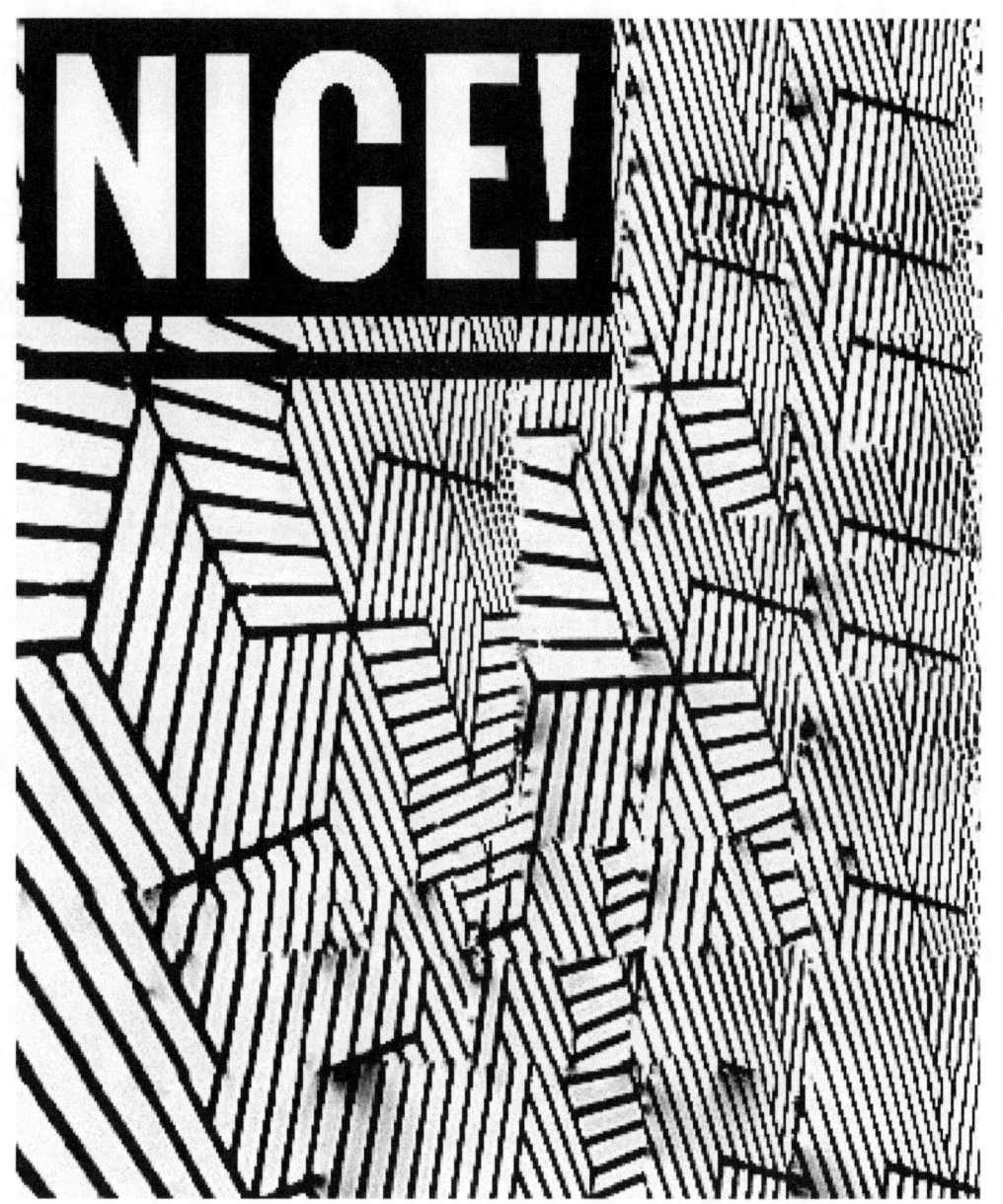

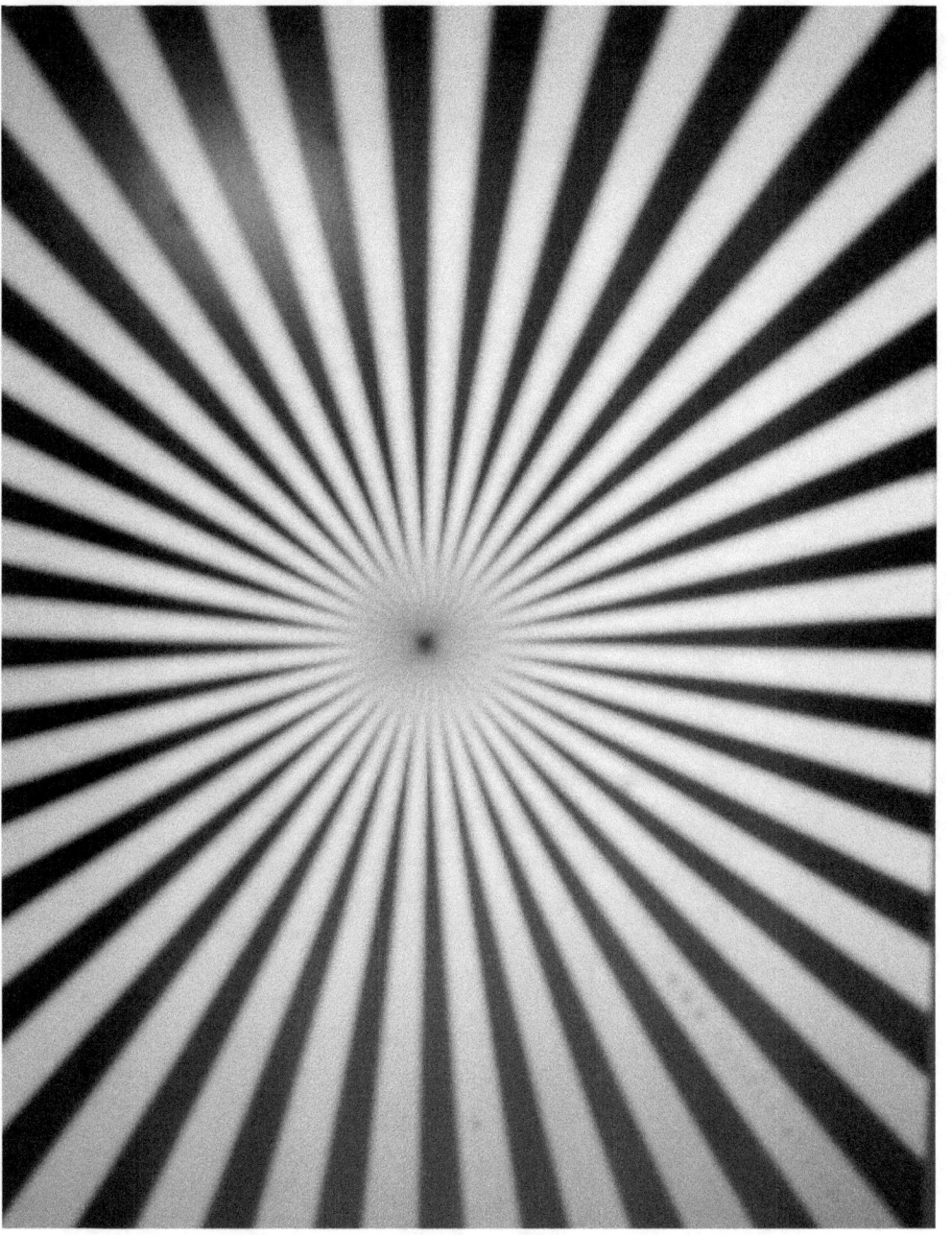

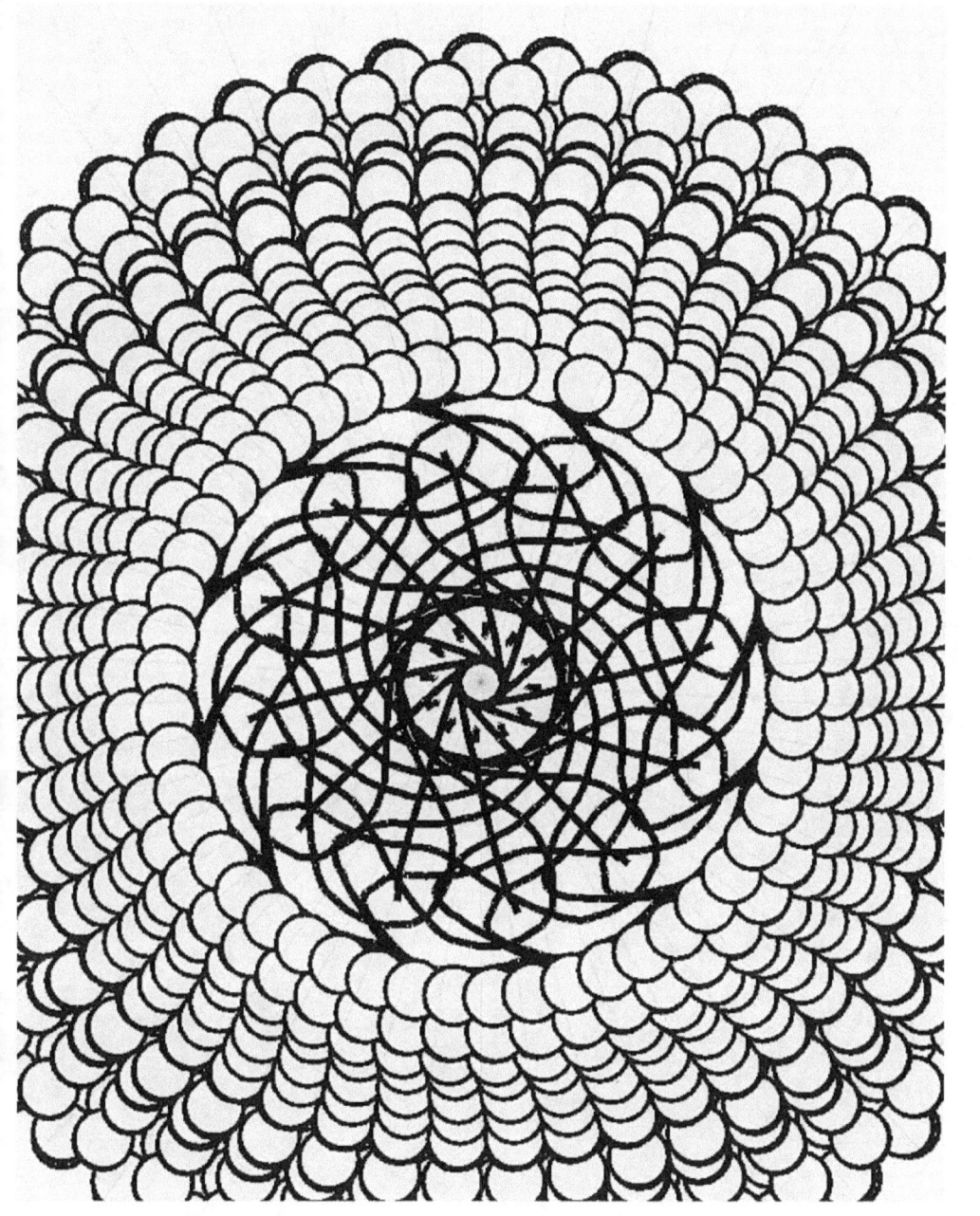

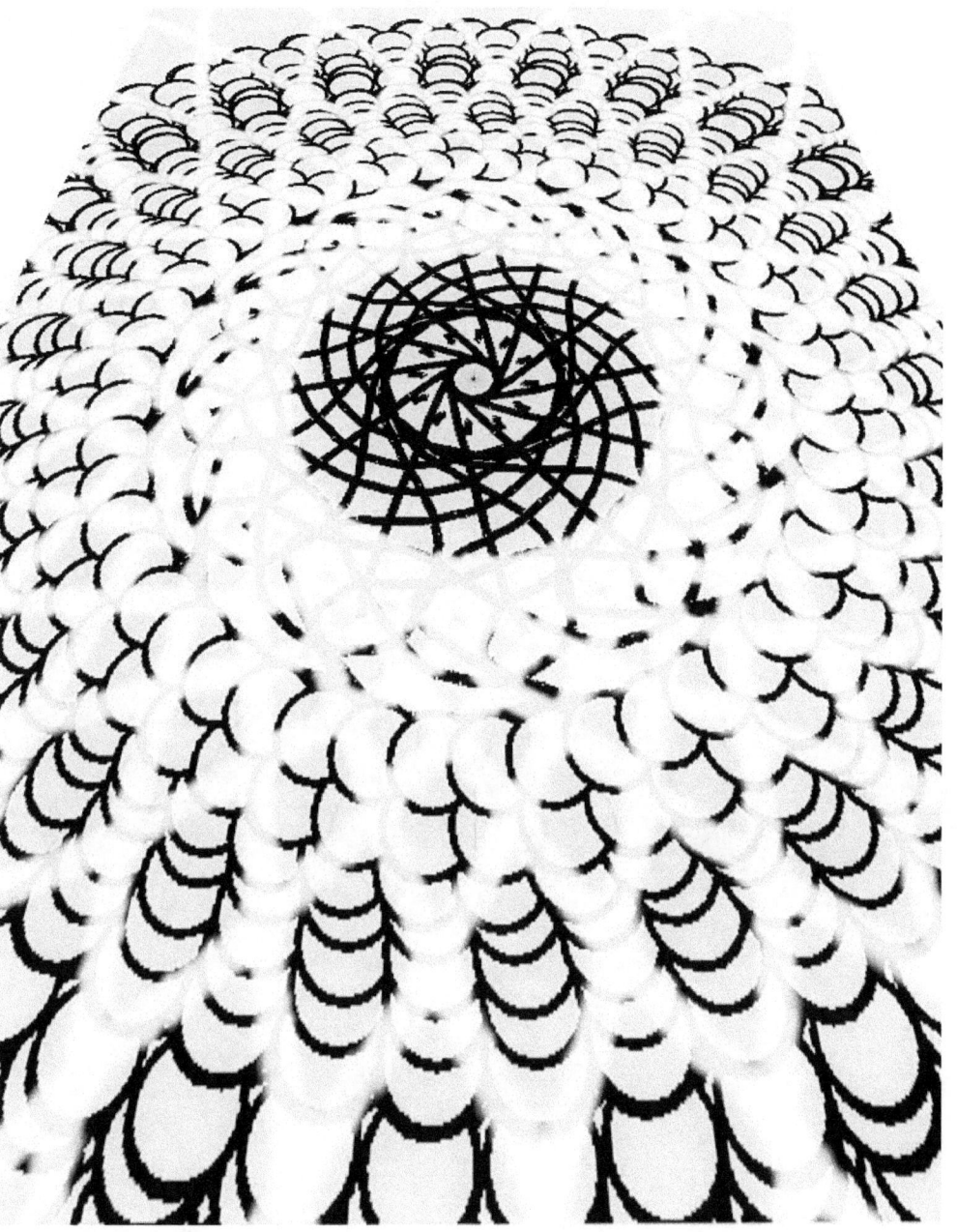

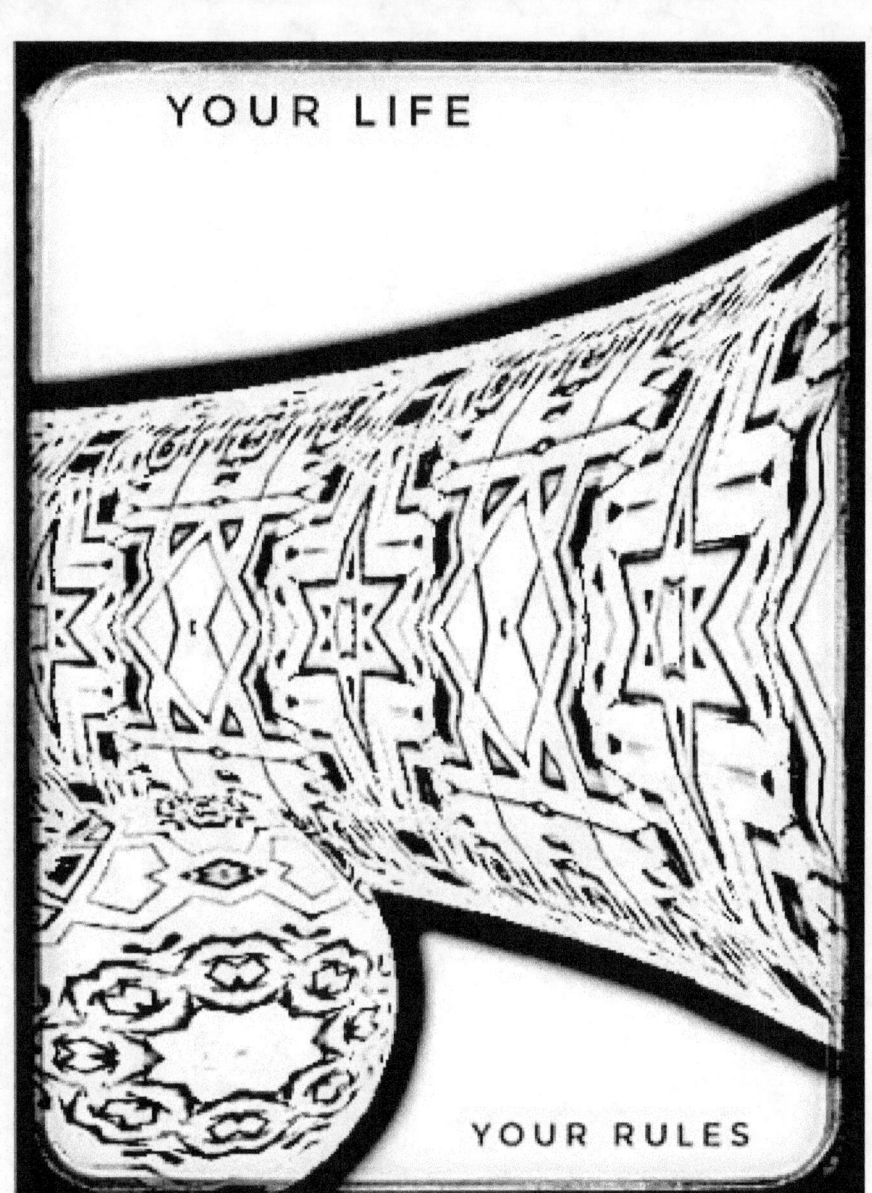

YOU ARE

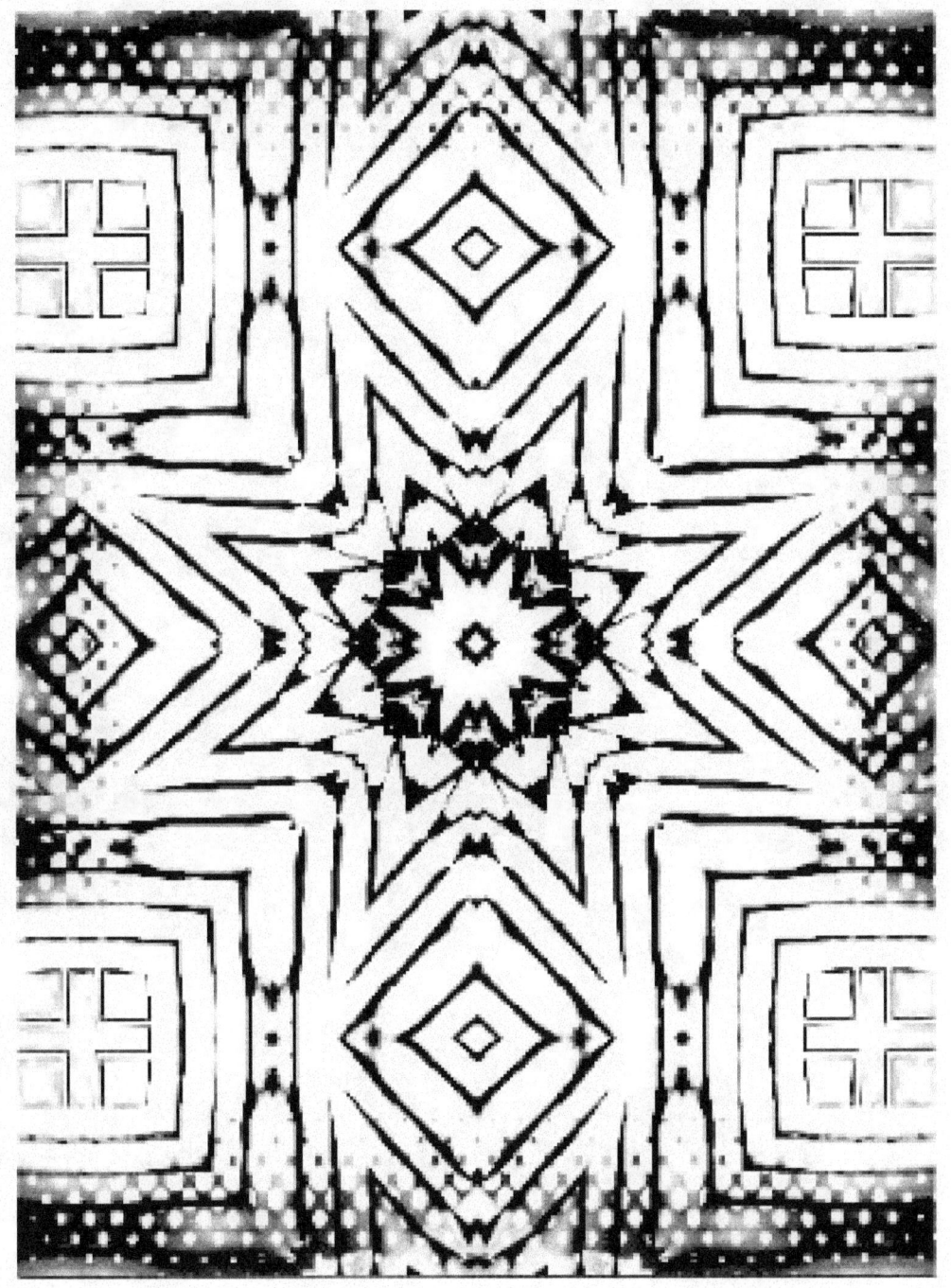

BEYOND LIMIT

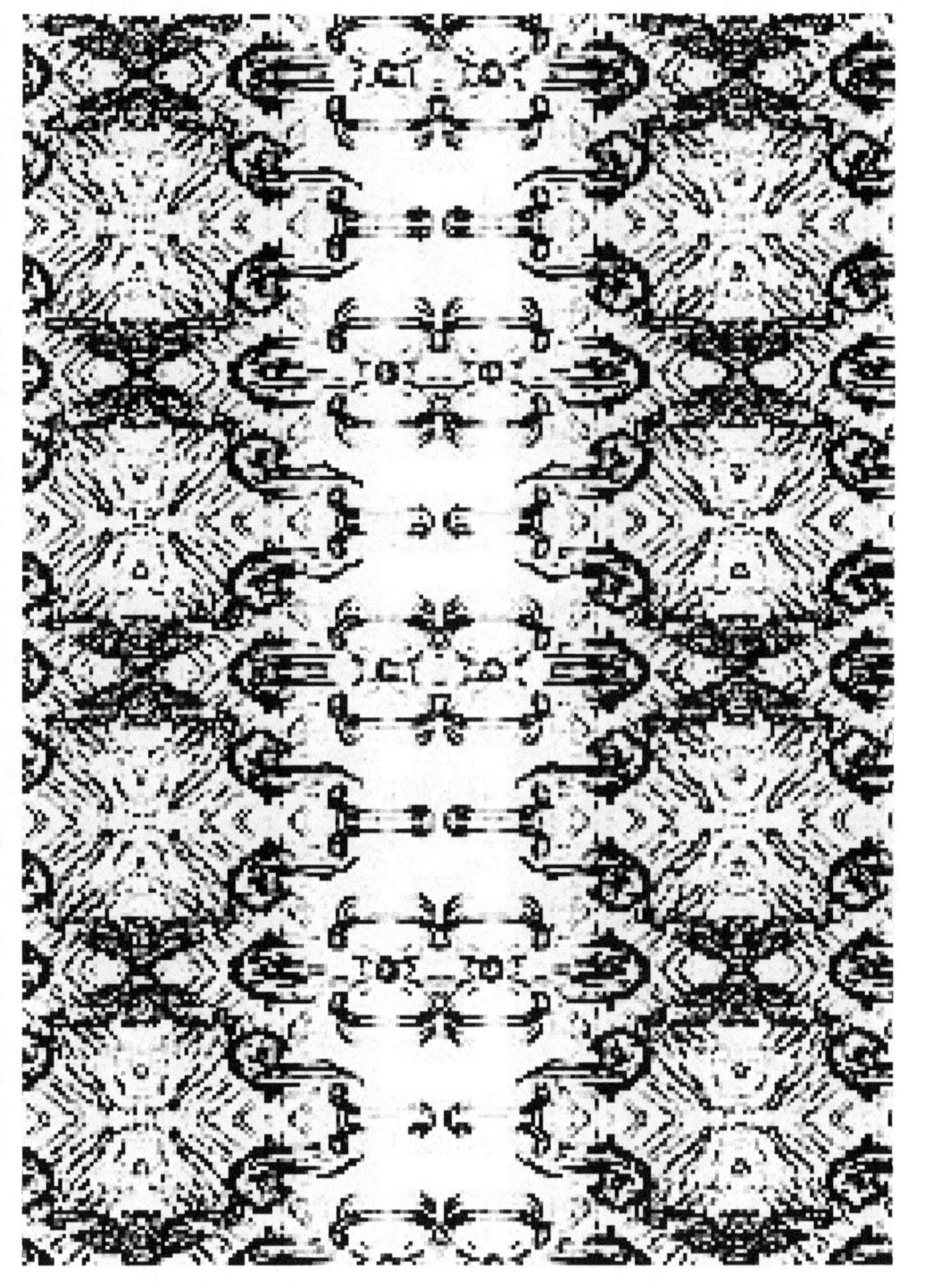

YOU CAN CHANGE

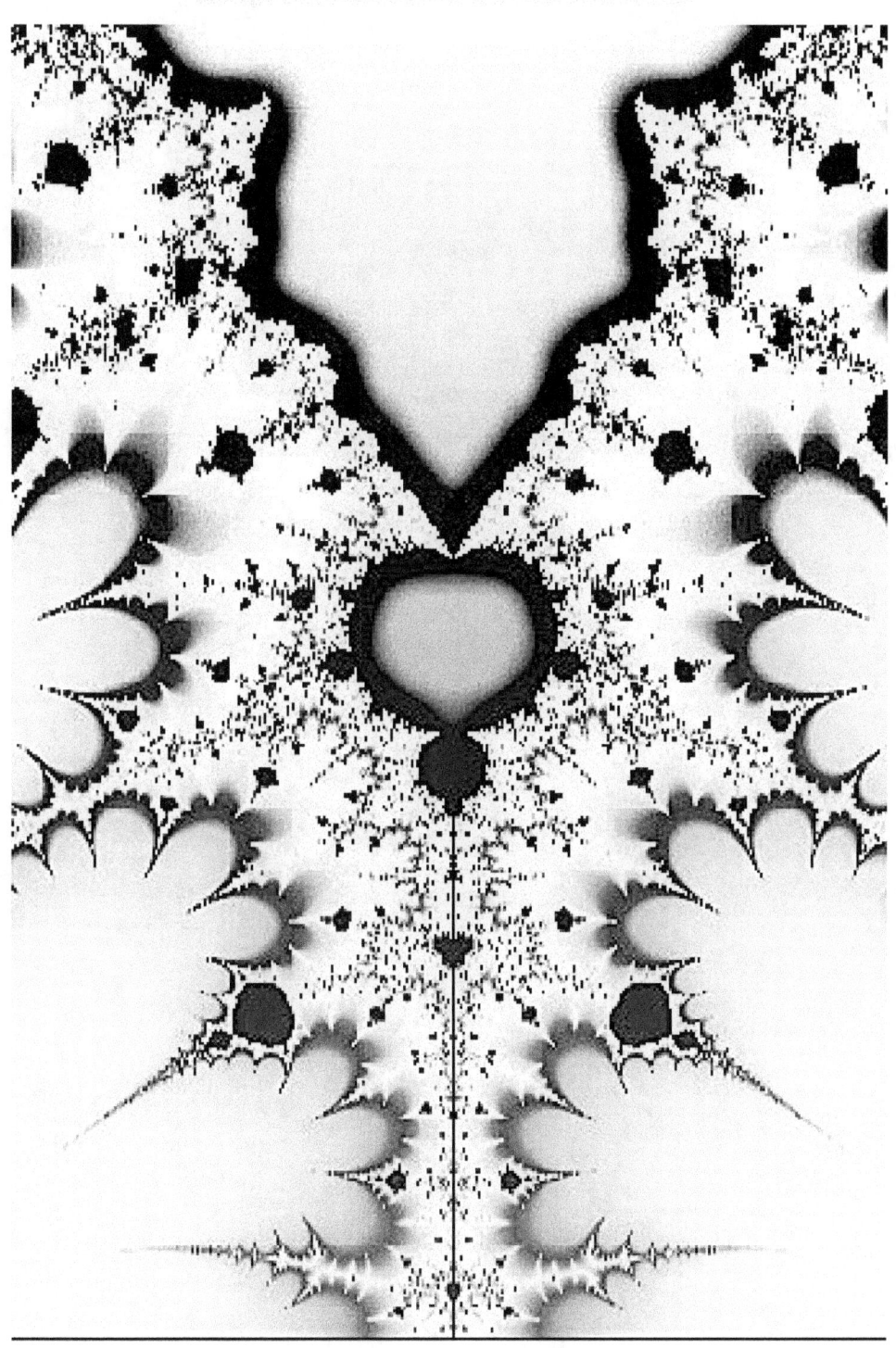

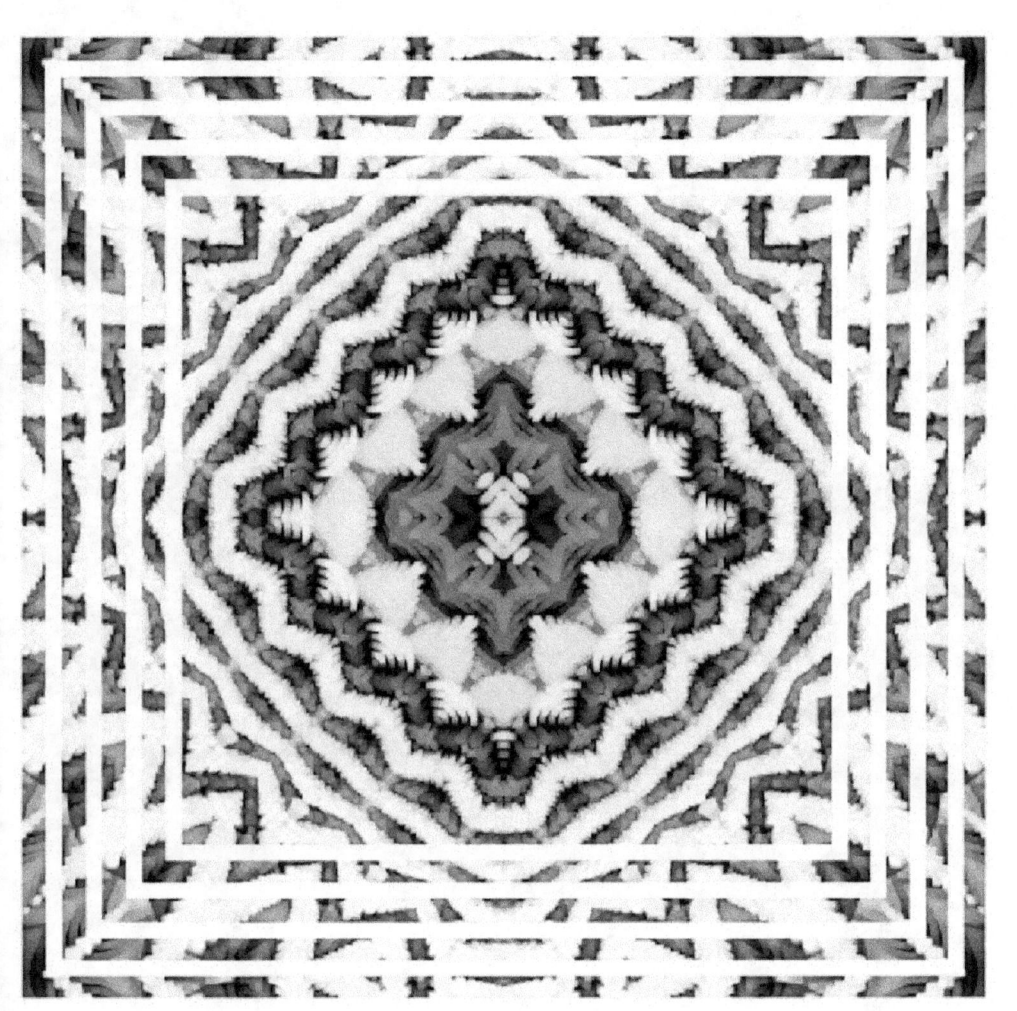

NOT A PROBLEM

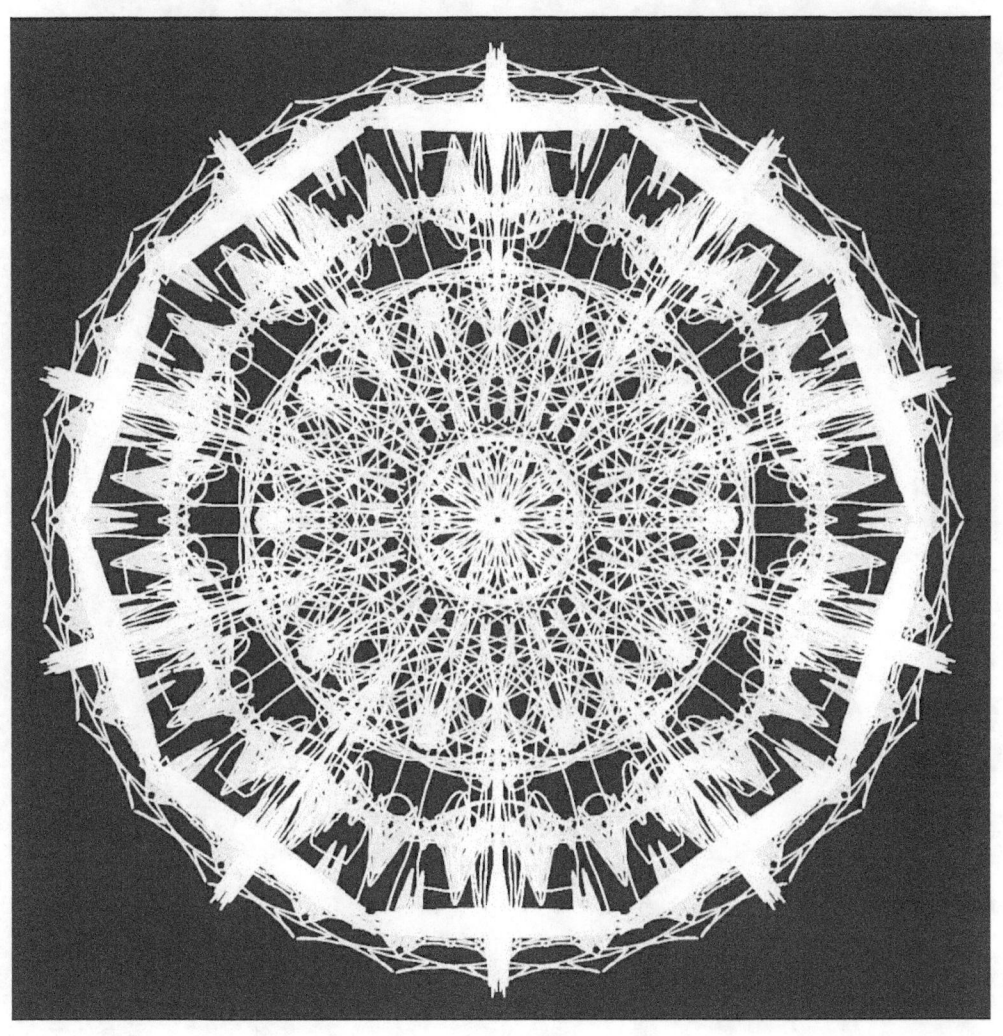

YOU MAKE

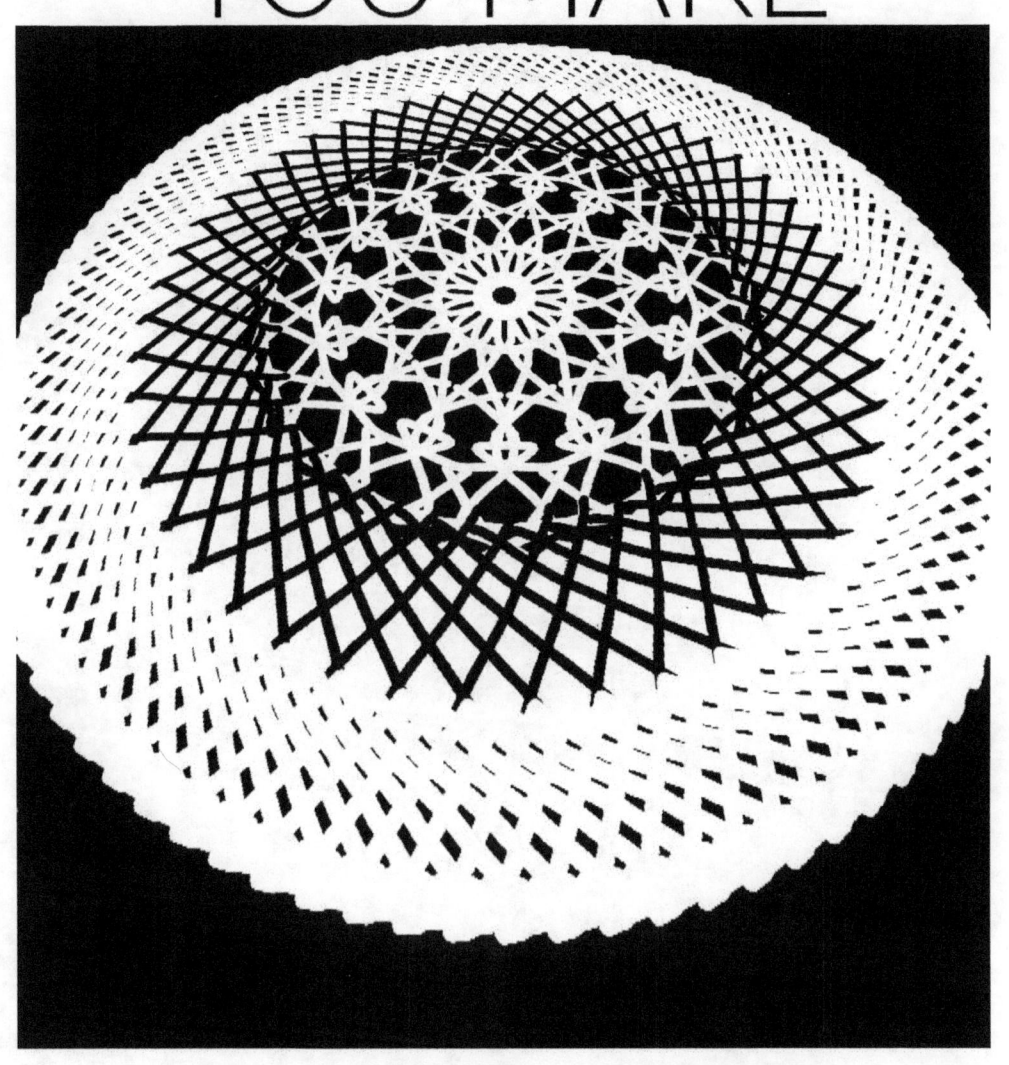

AMAZING HAPPEN

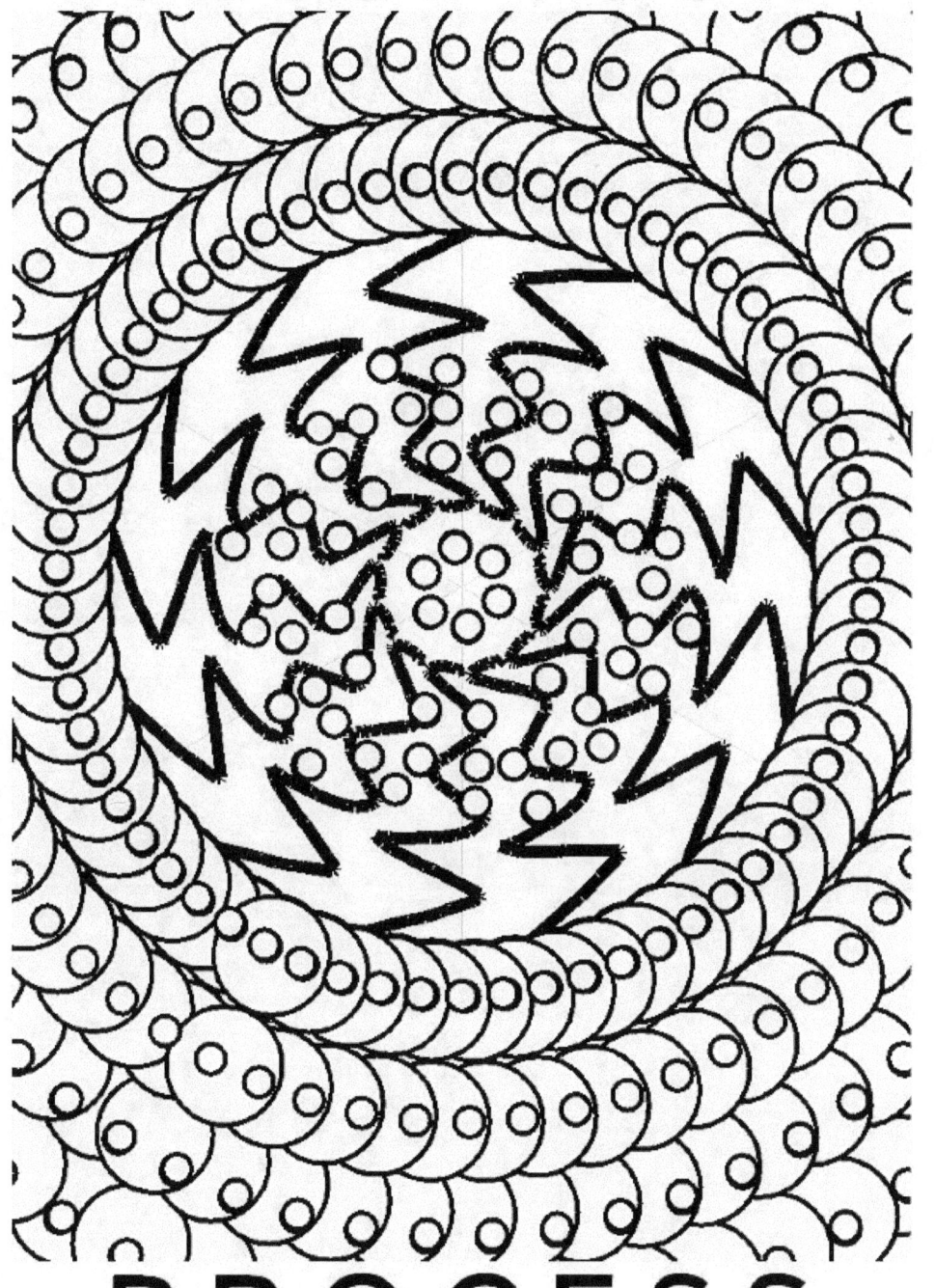

KNOW YOU CAN

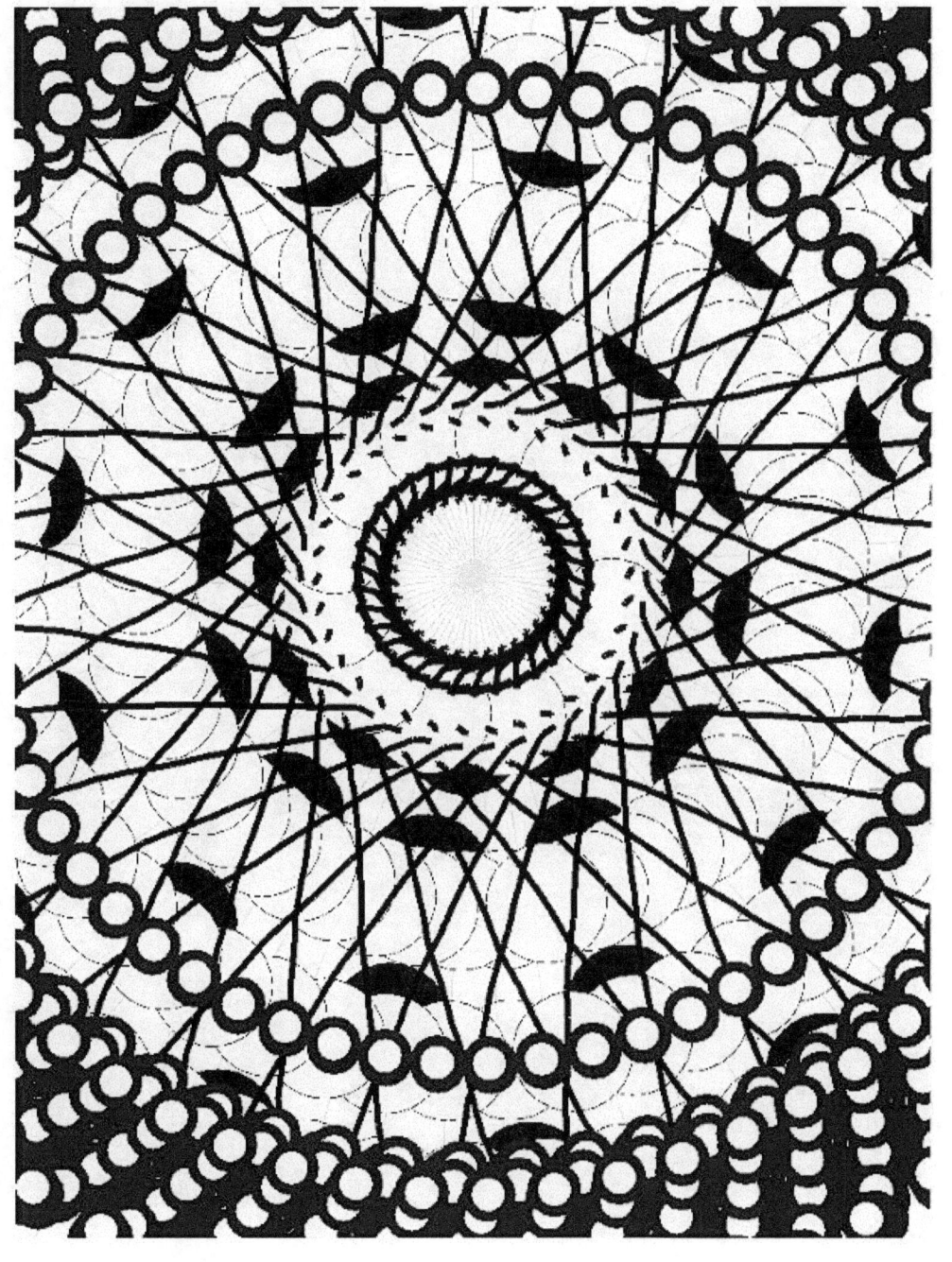

NOT ALL
WANDERERS
ARE LOST

BEING YOU

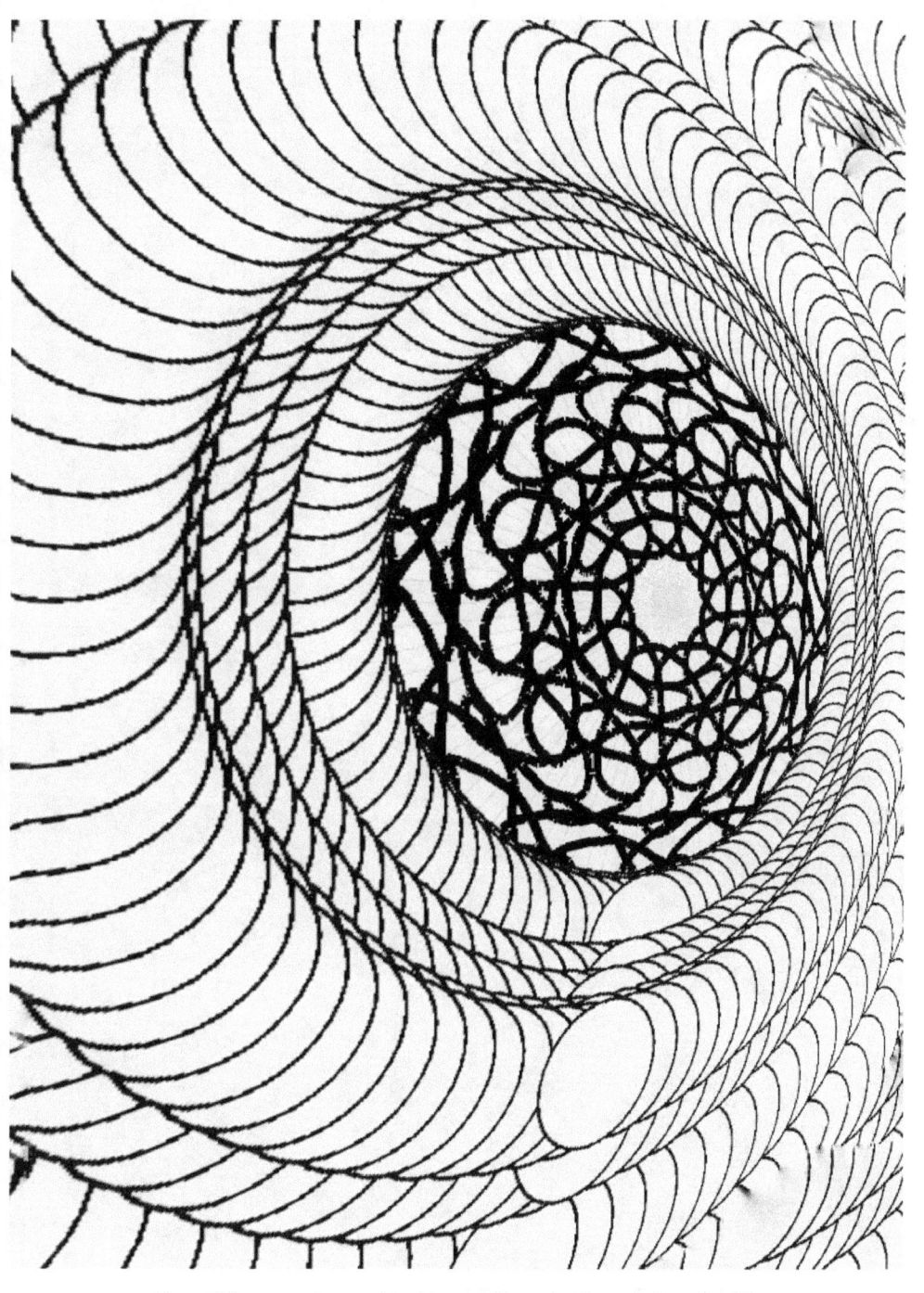

IS ENOUGH

BE FREE

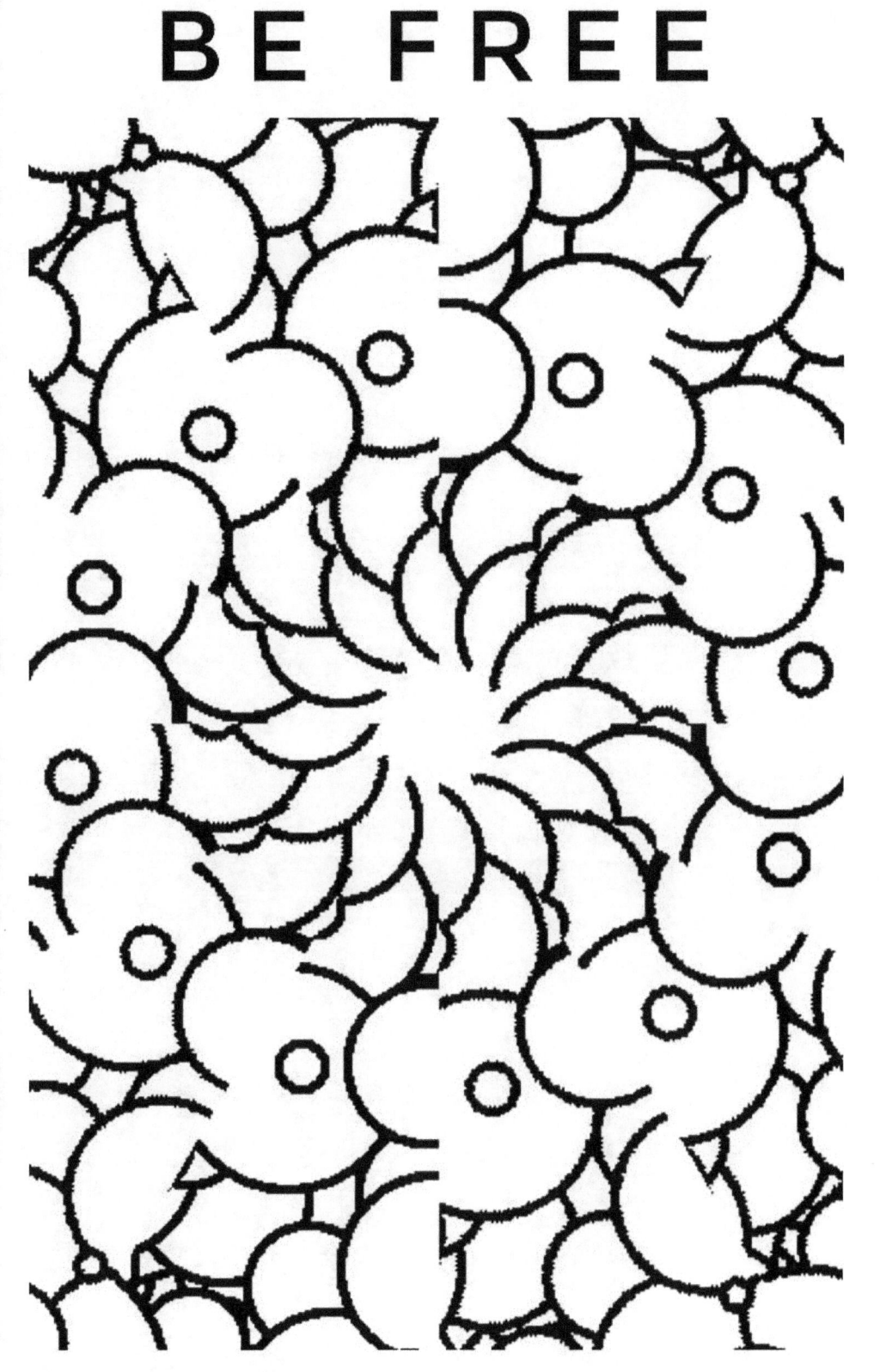

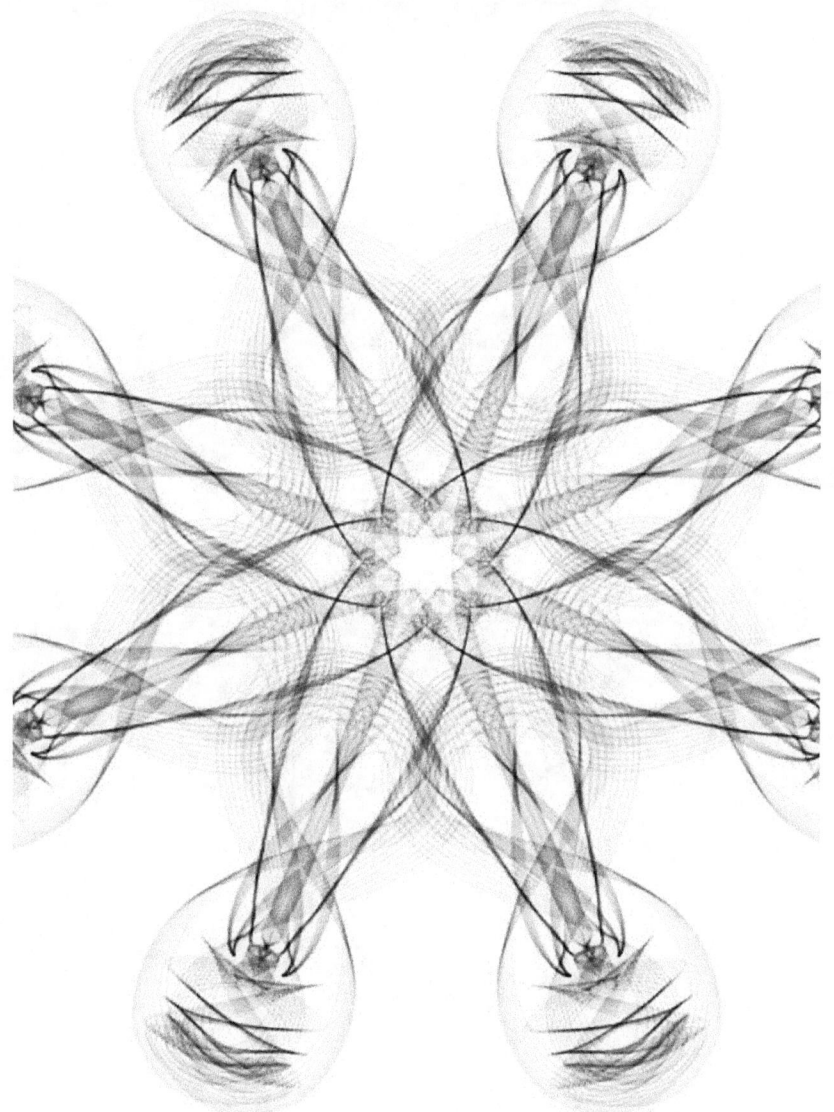

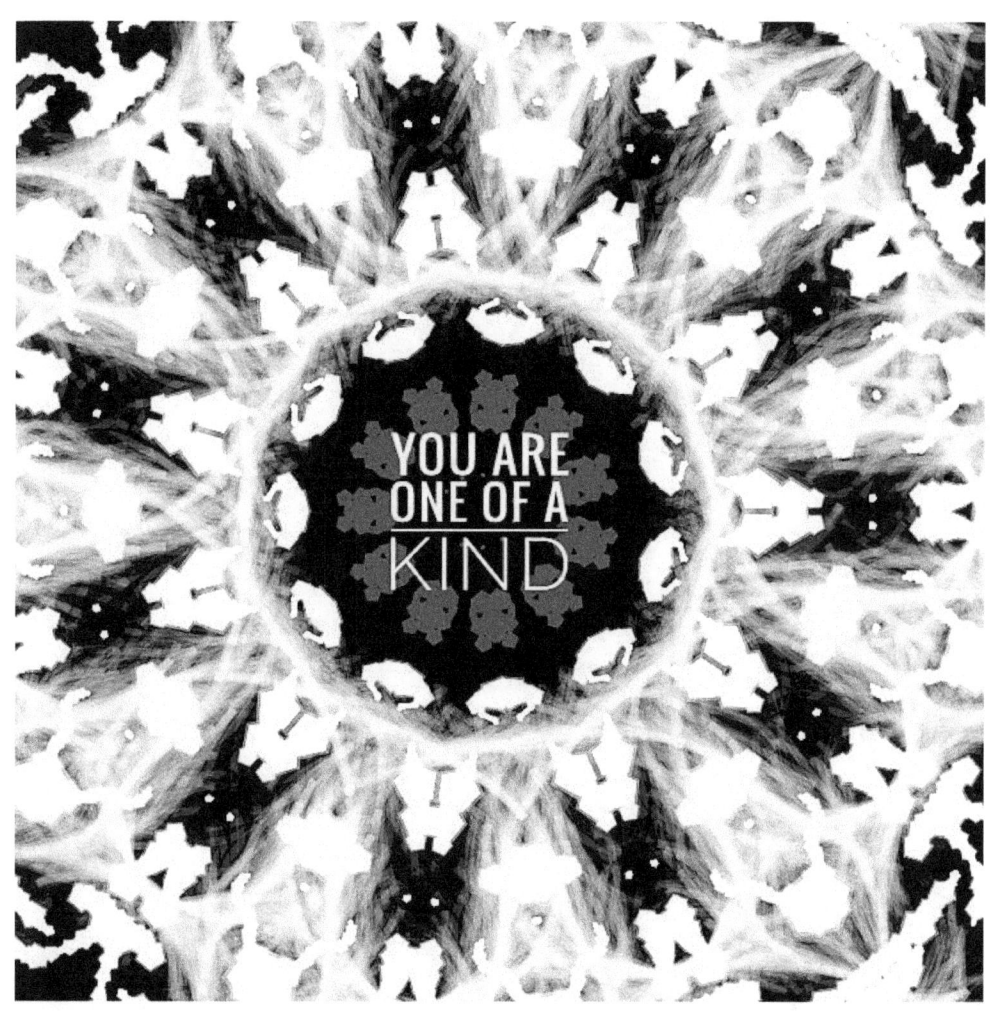

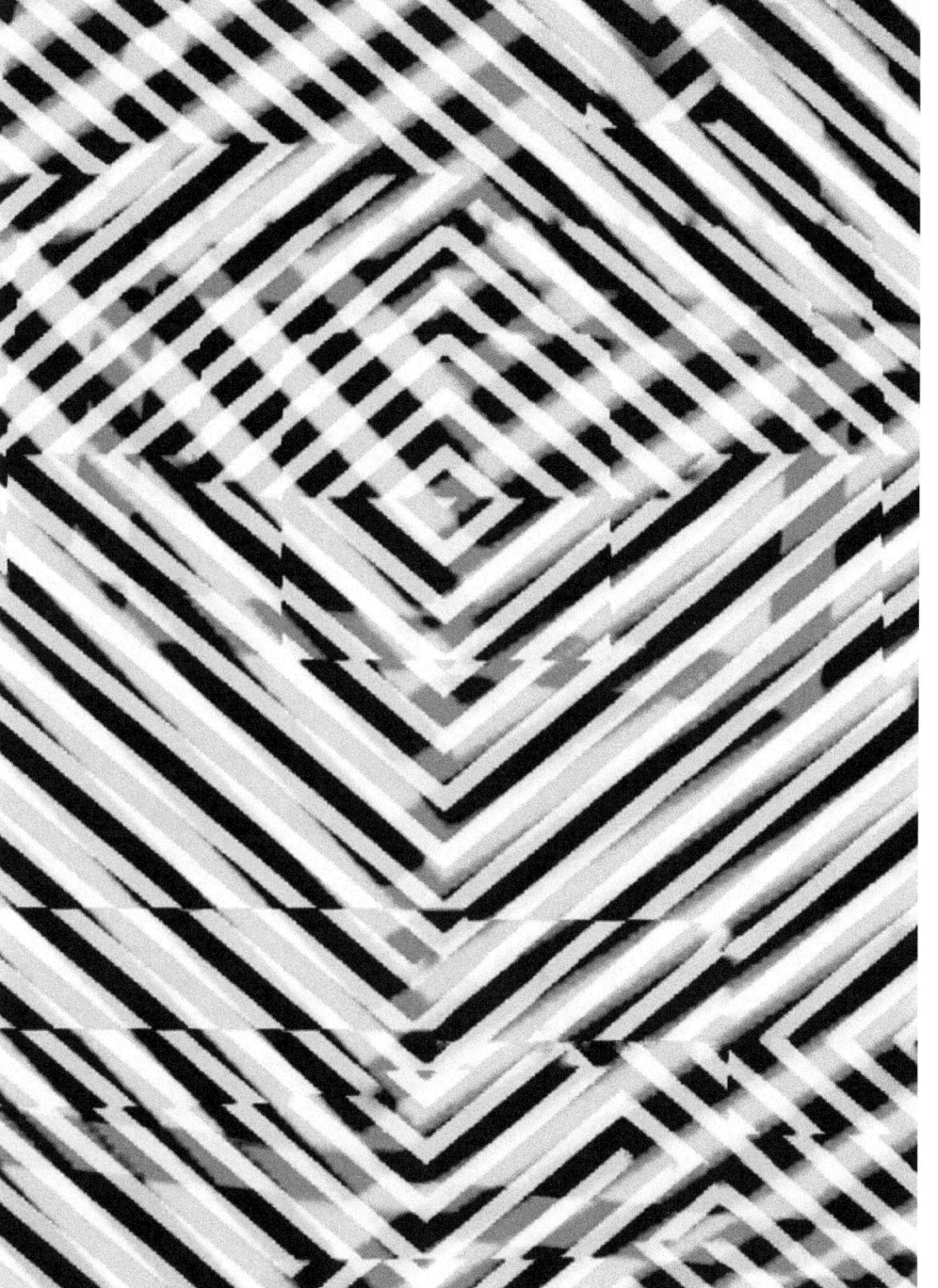

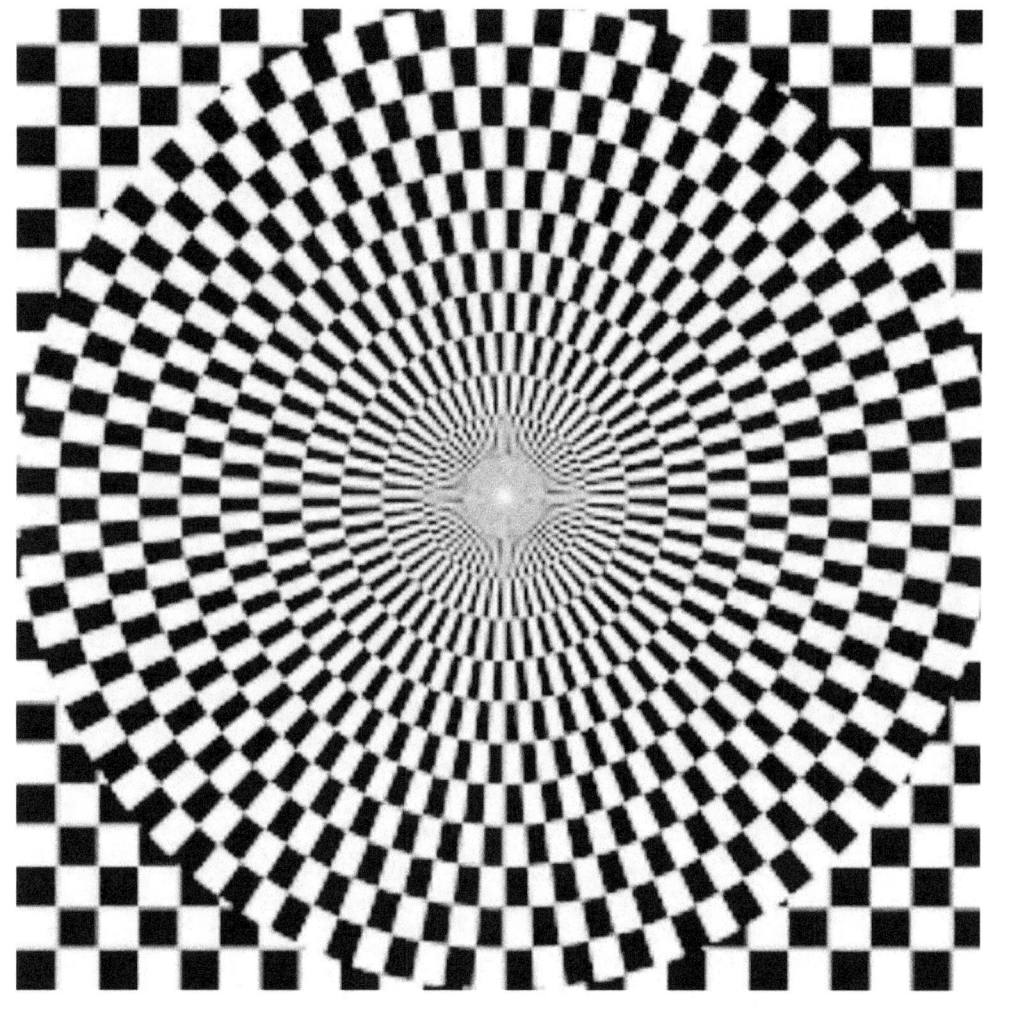

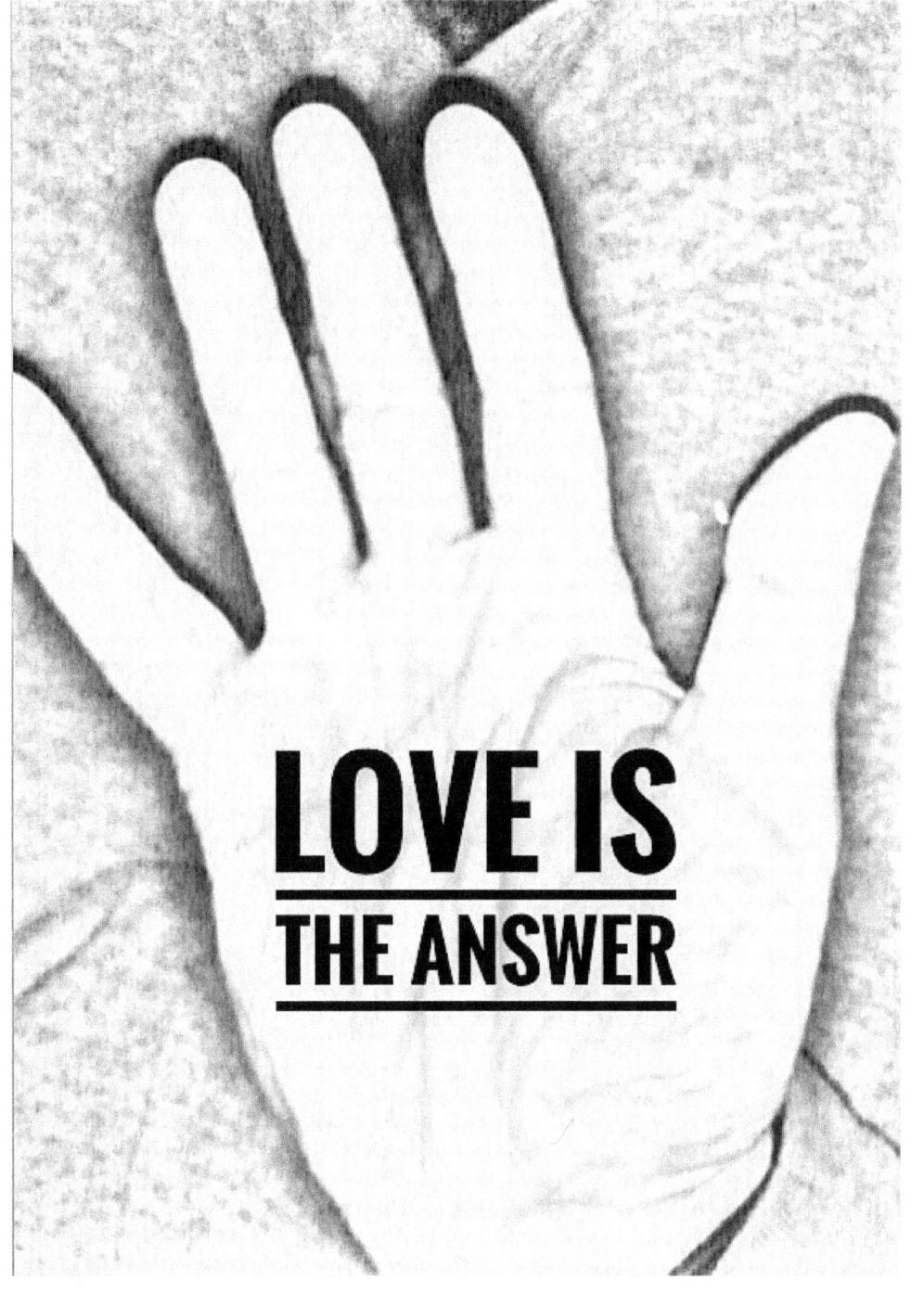

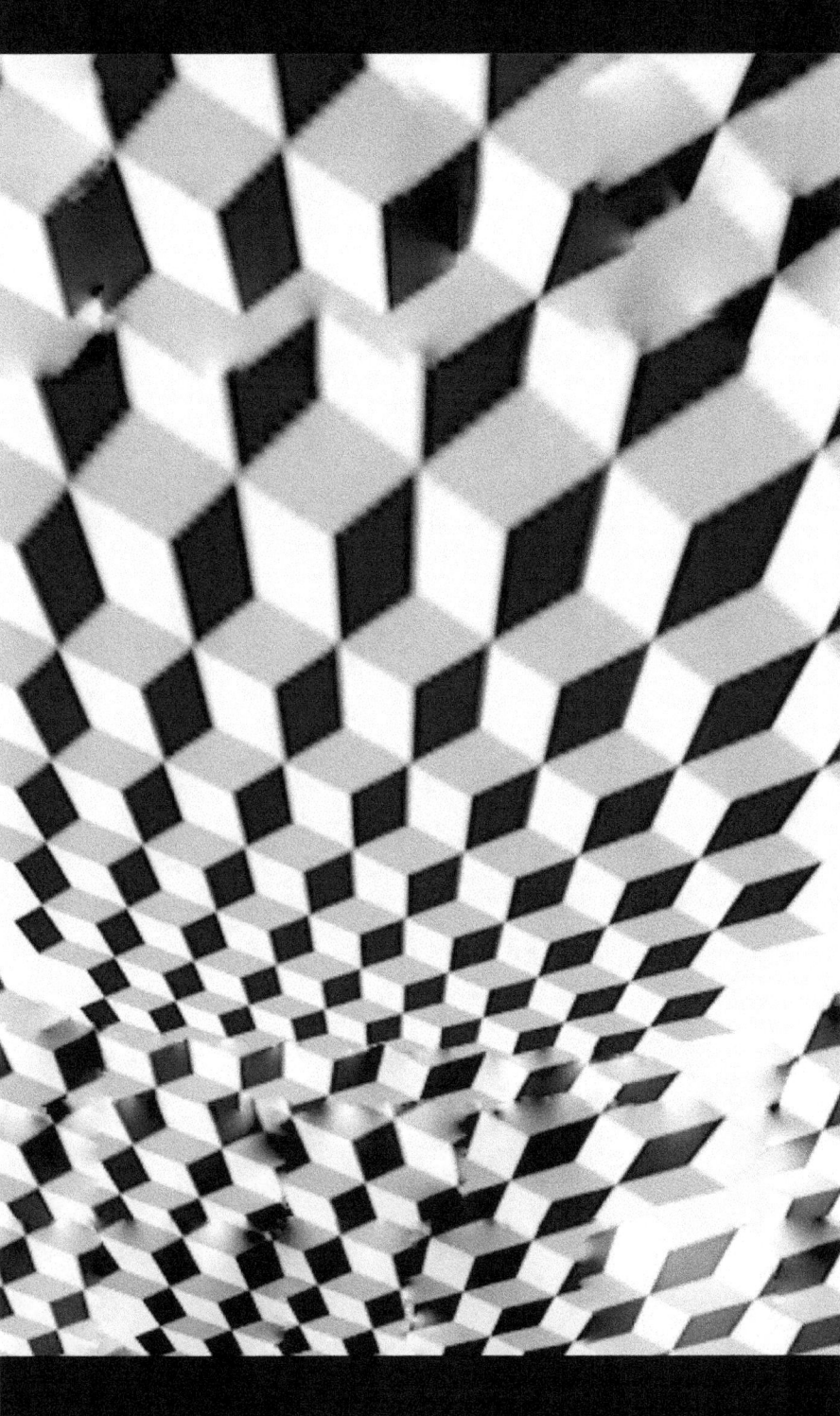

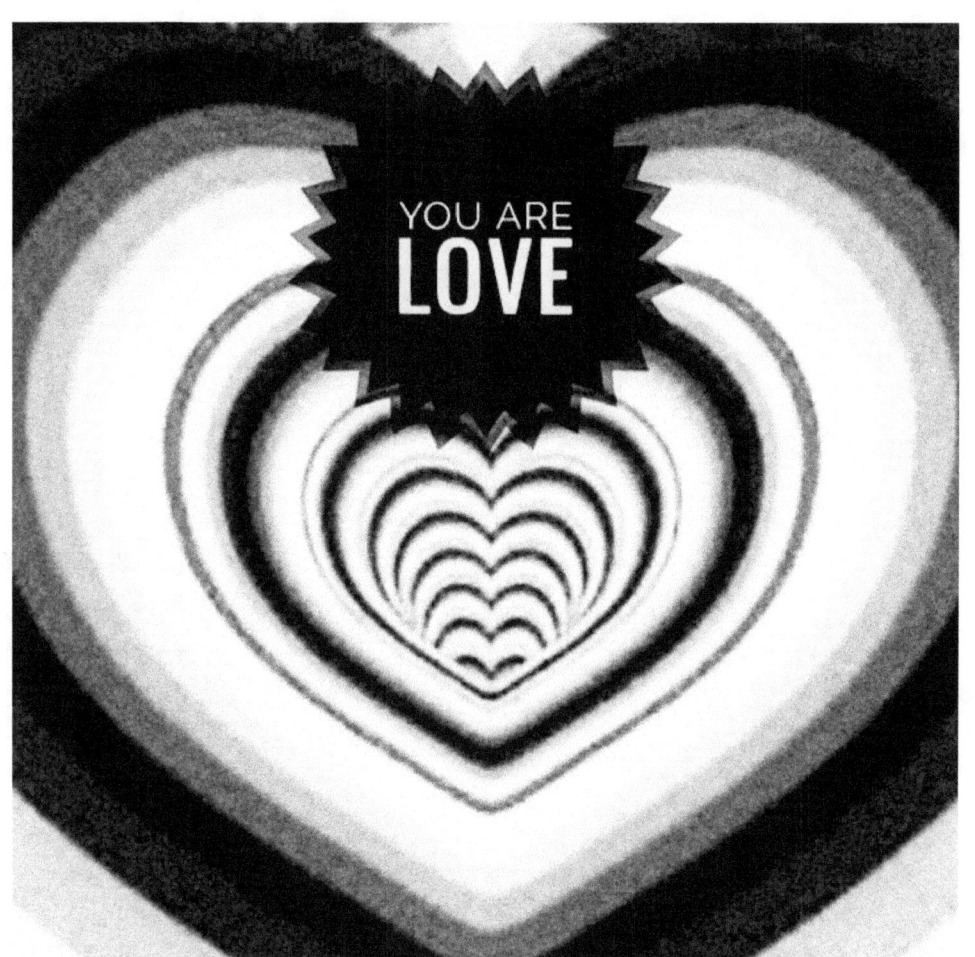

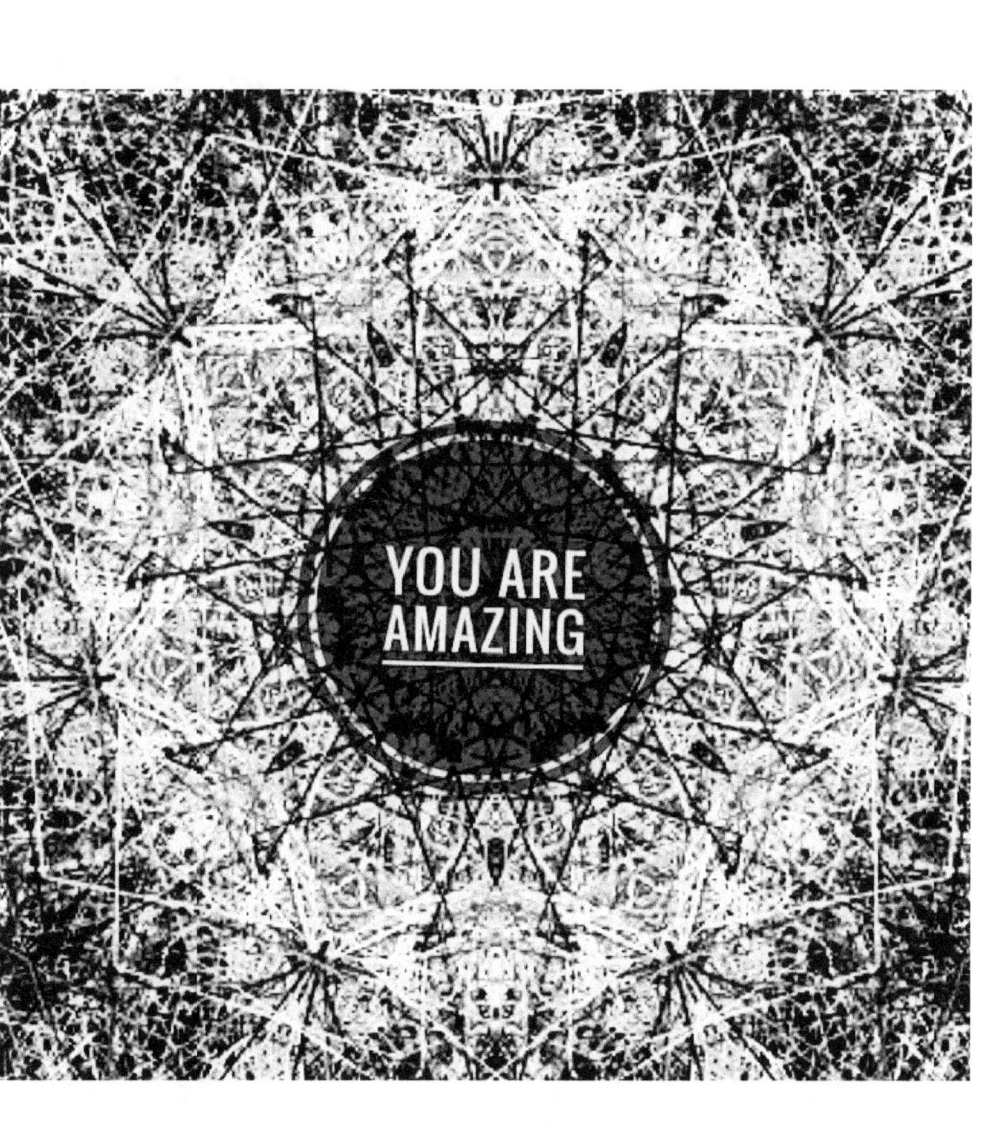

EMBRACE

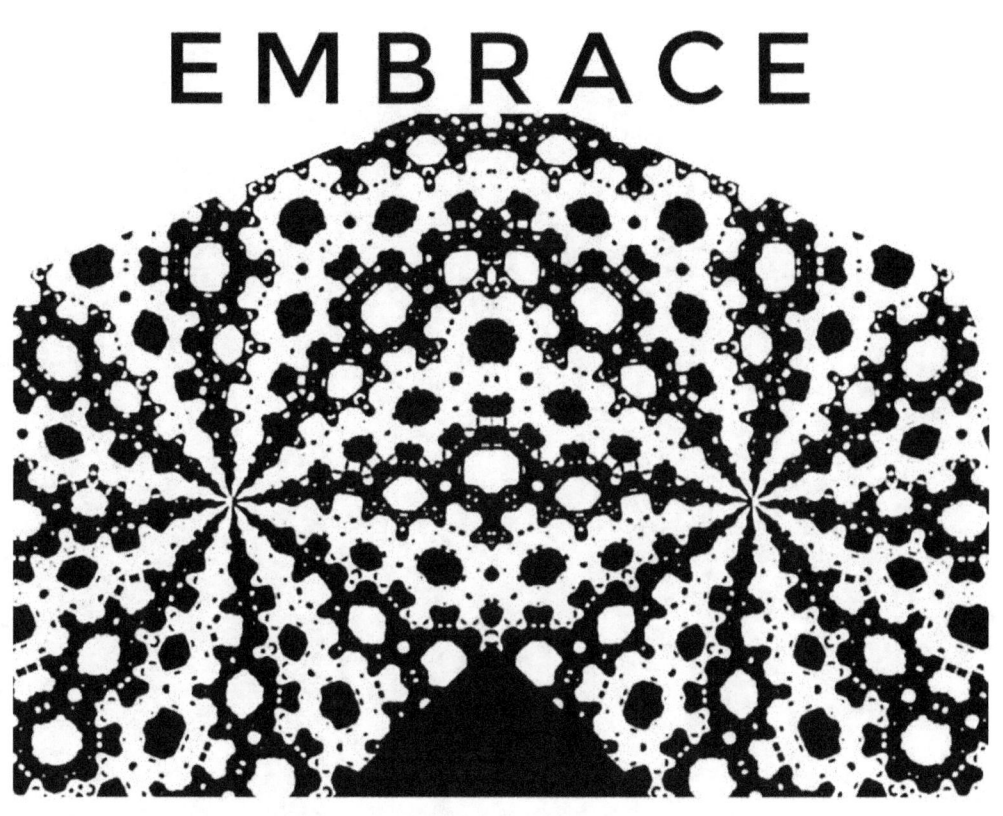

GRATITUDE

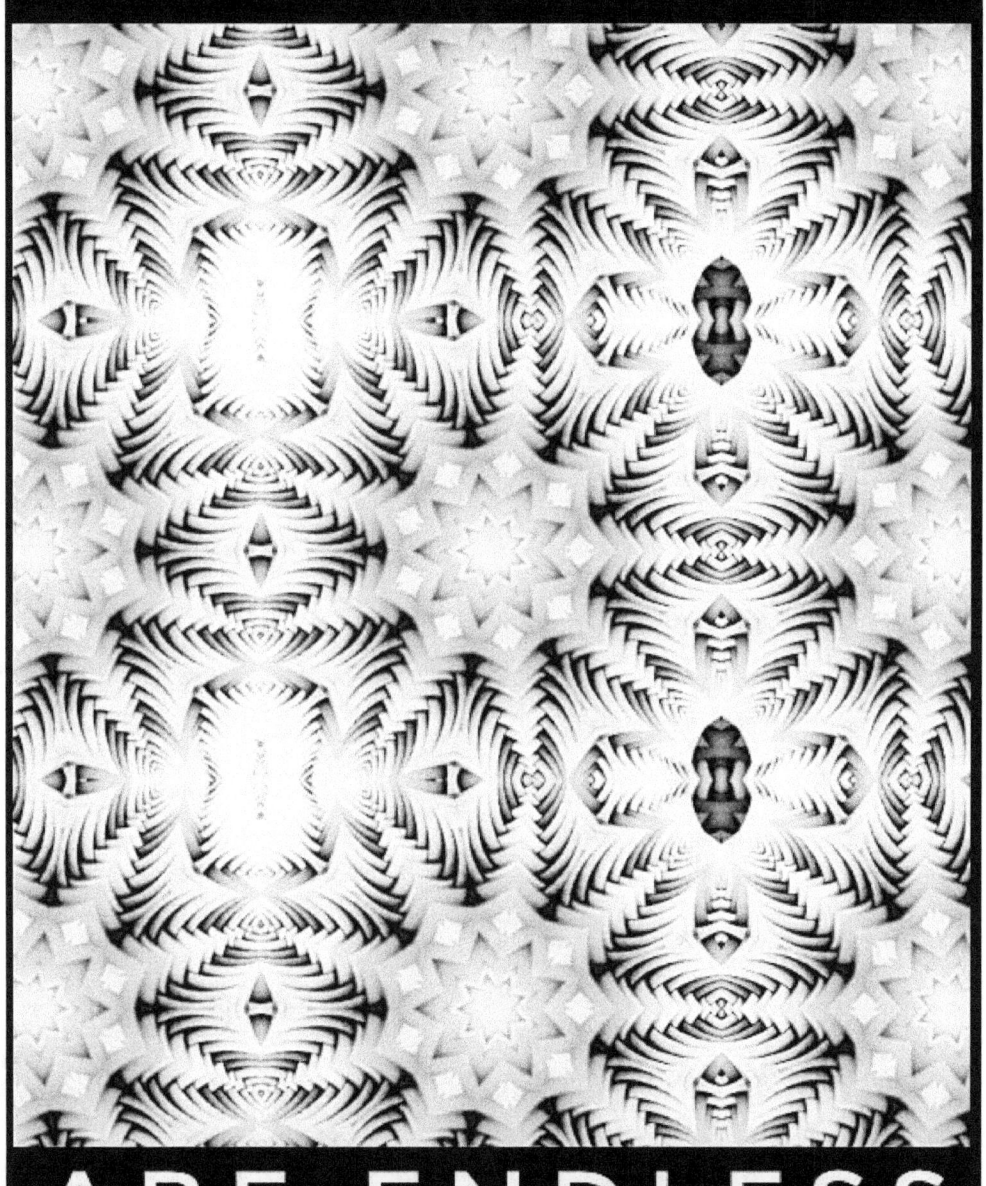

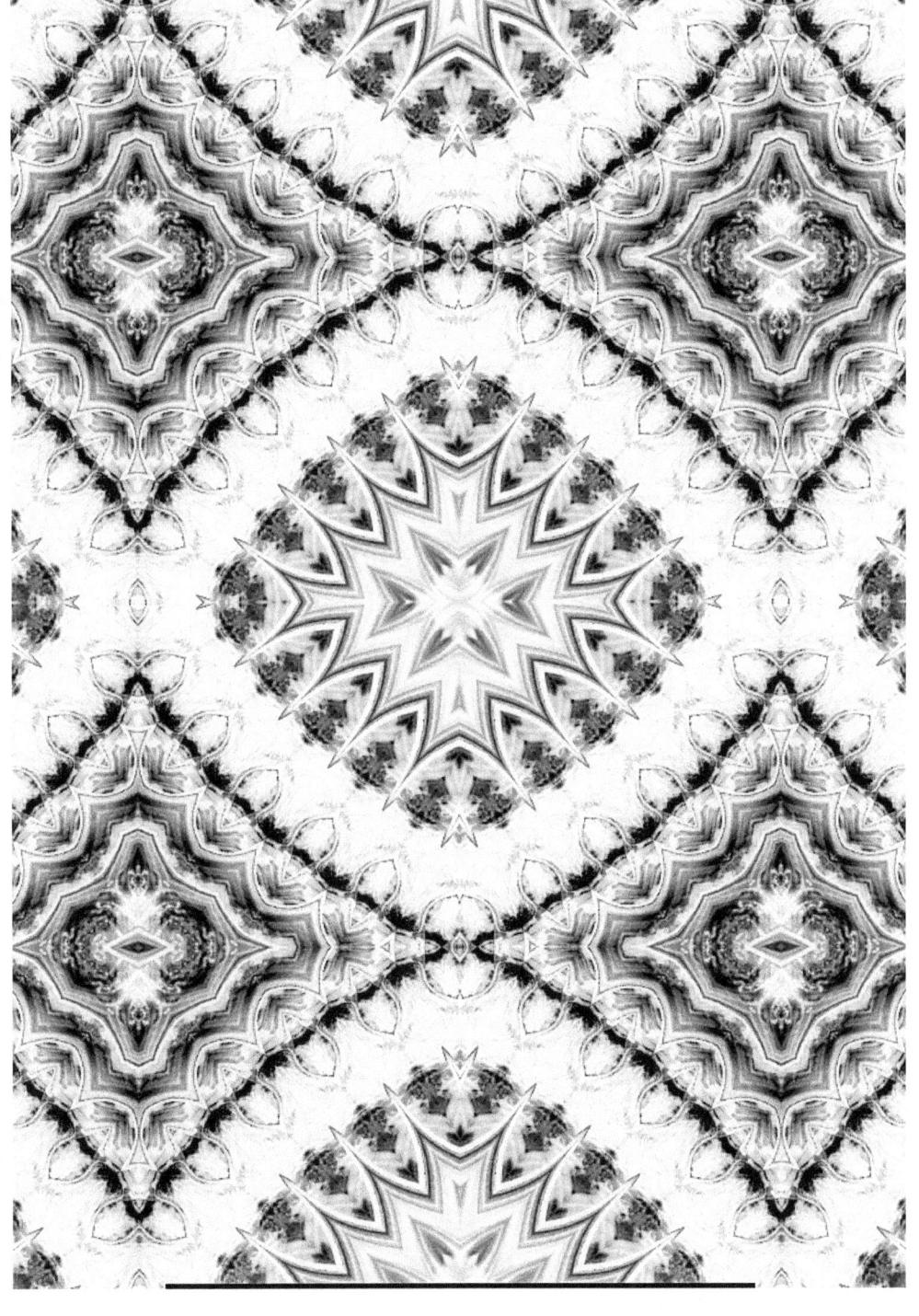

BUILD A BETTER

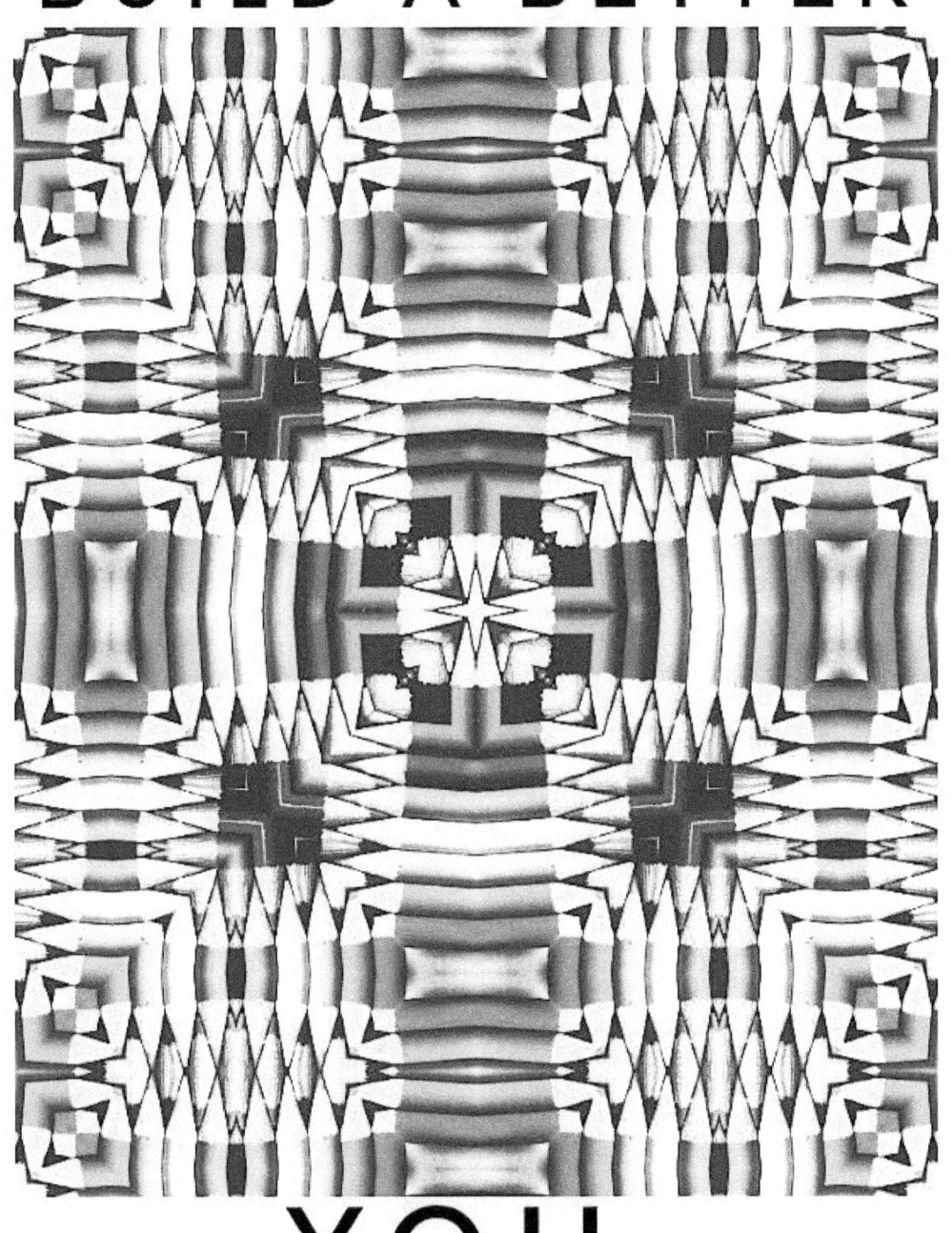

YOU

ALL THIS IS

FOR YOU

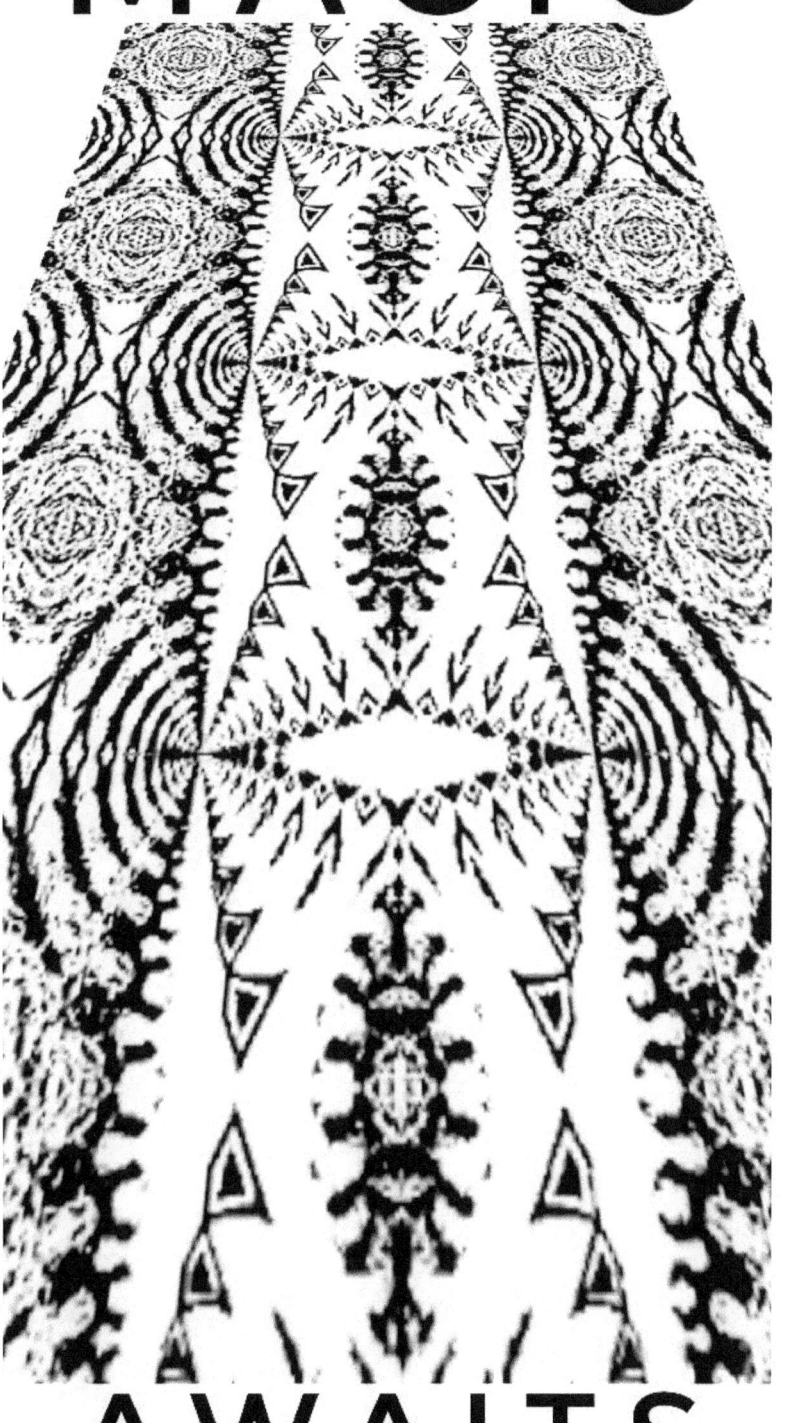

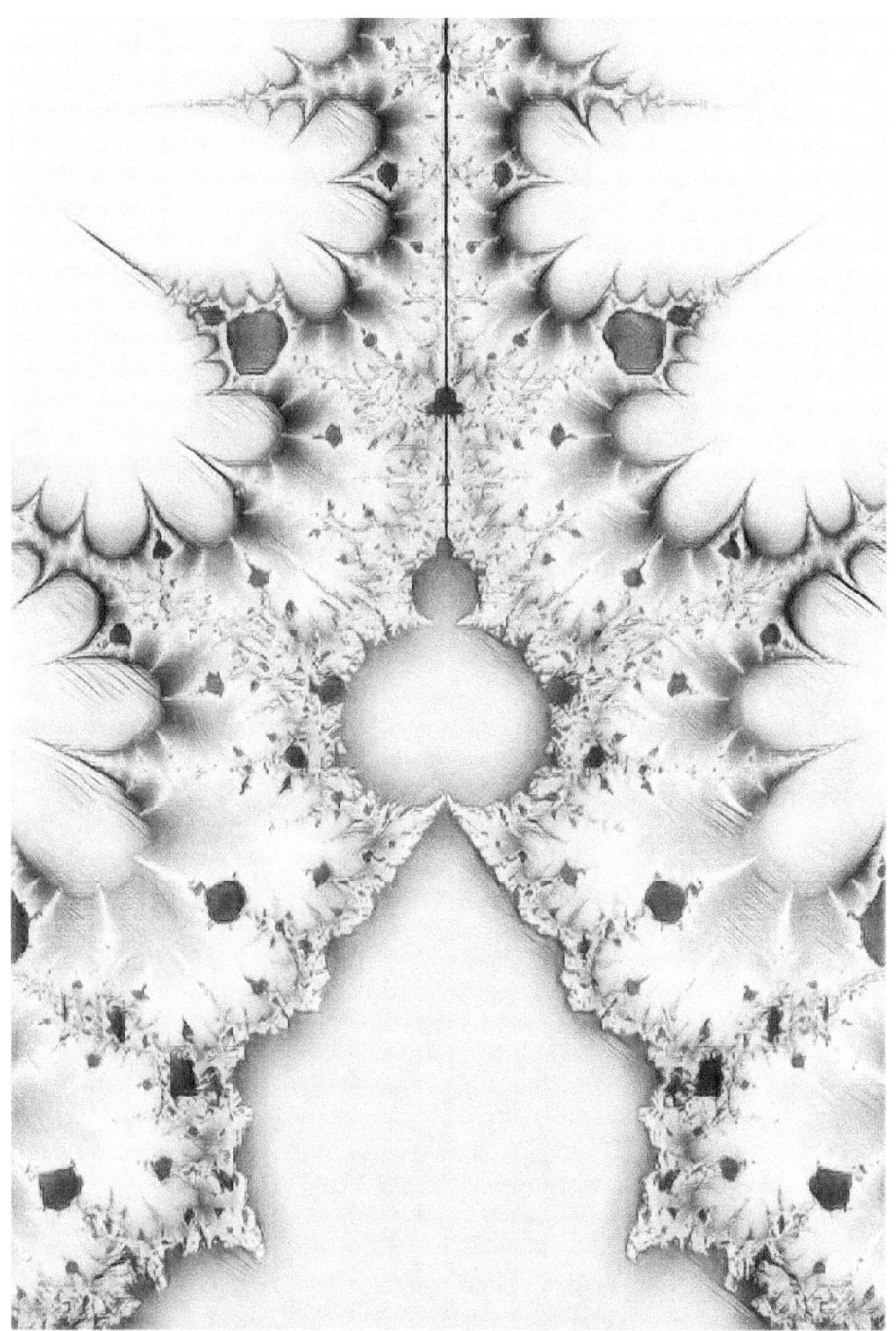

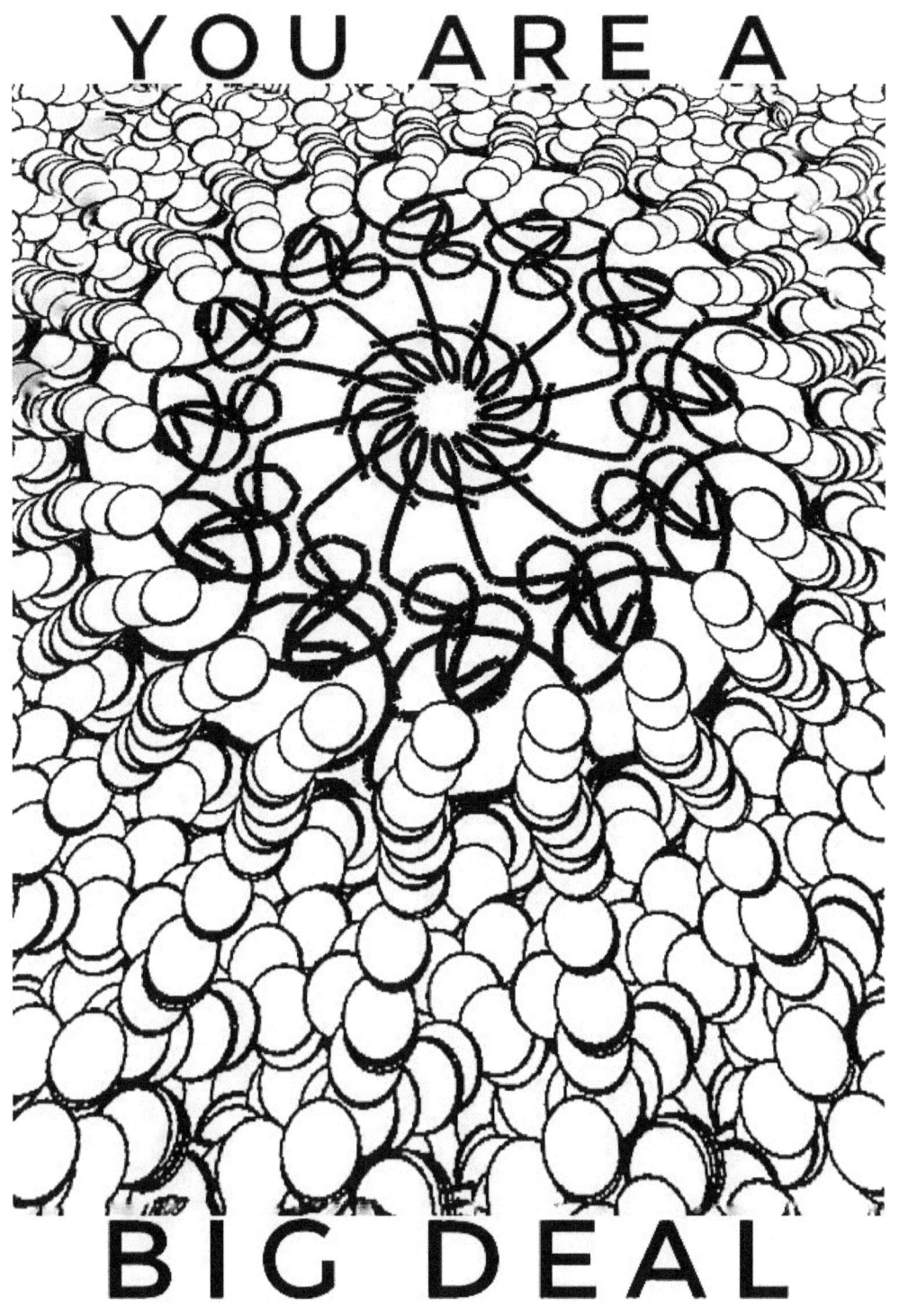

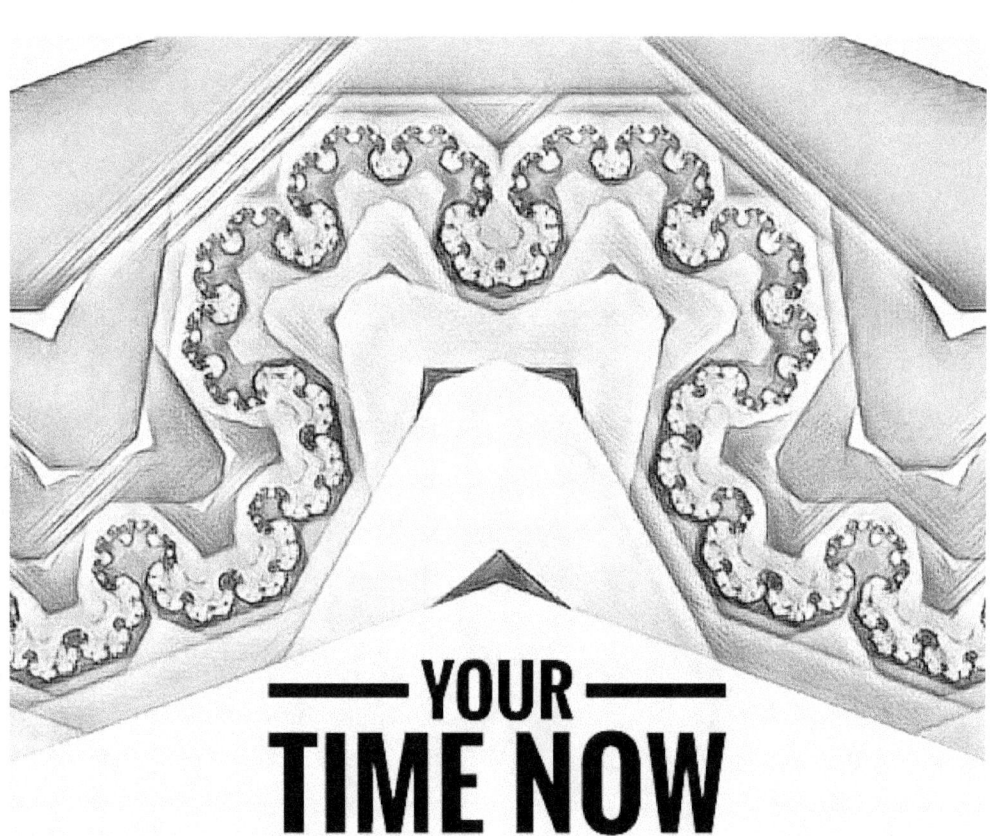

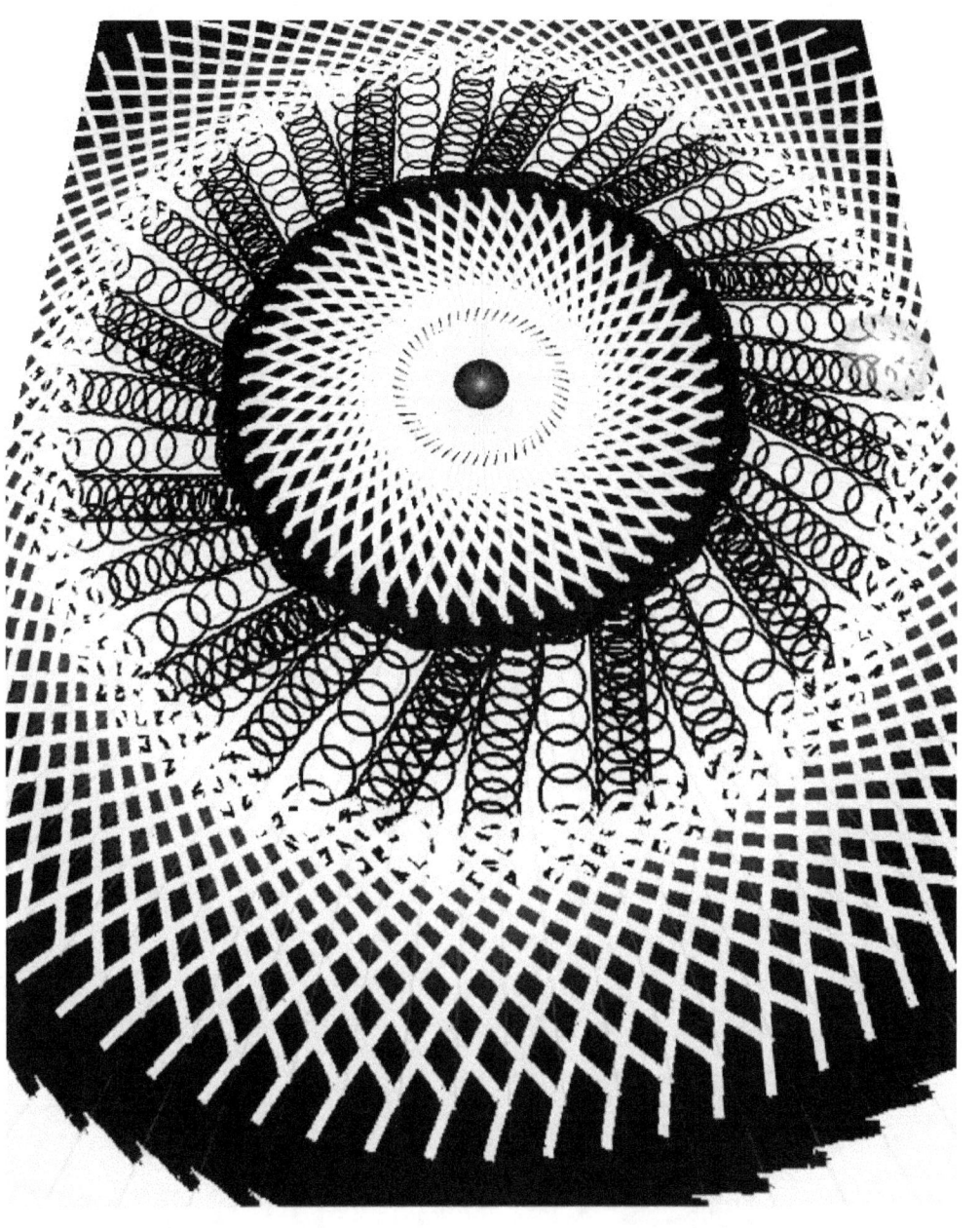

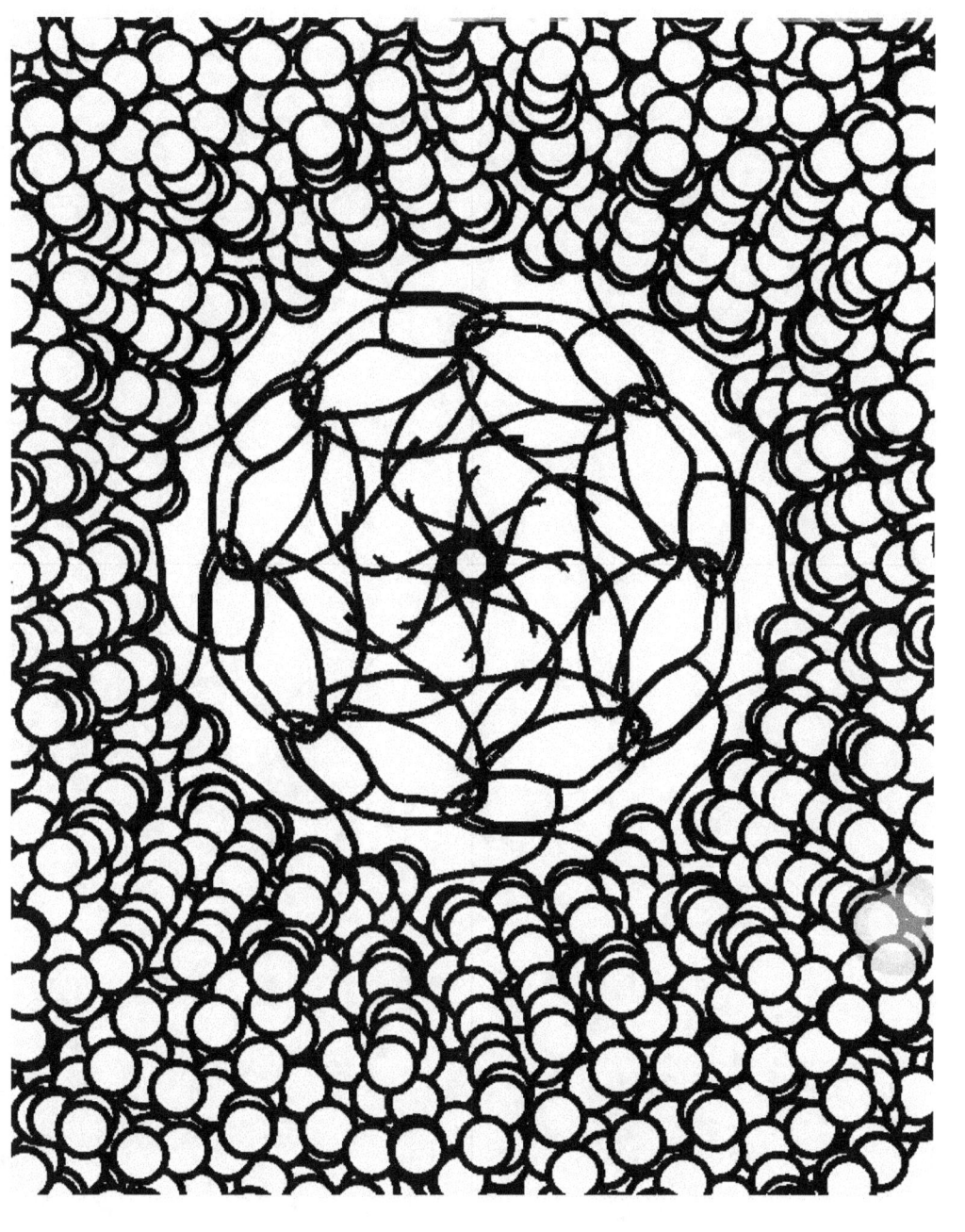

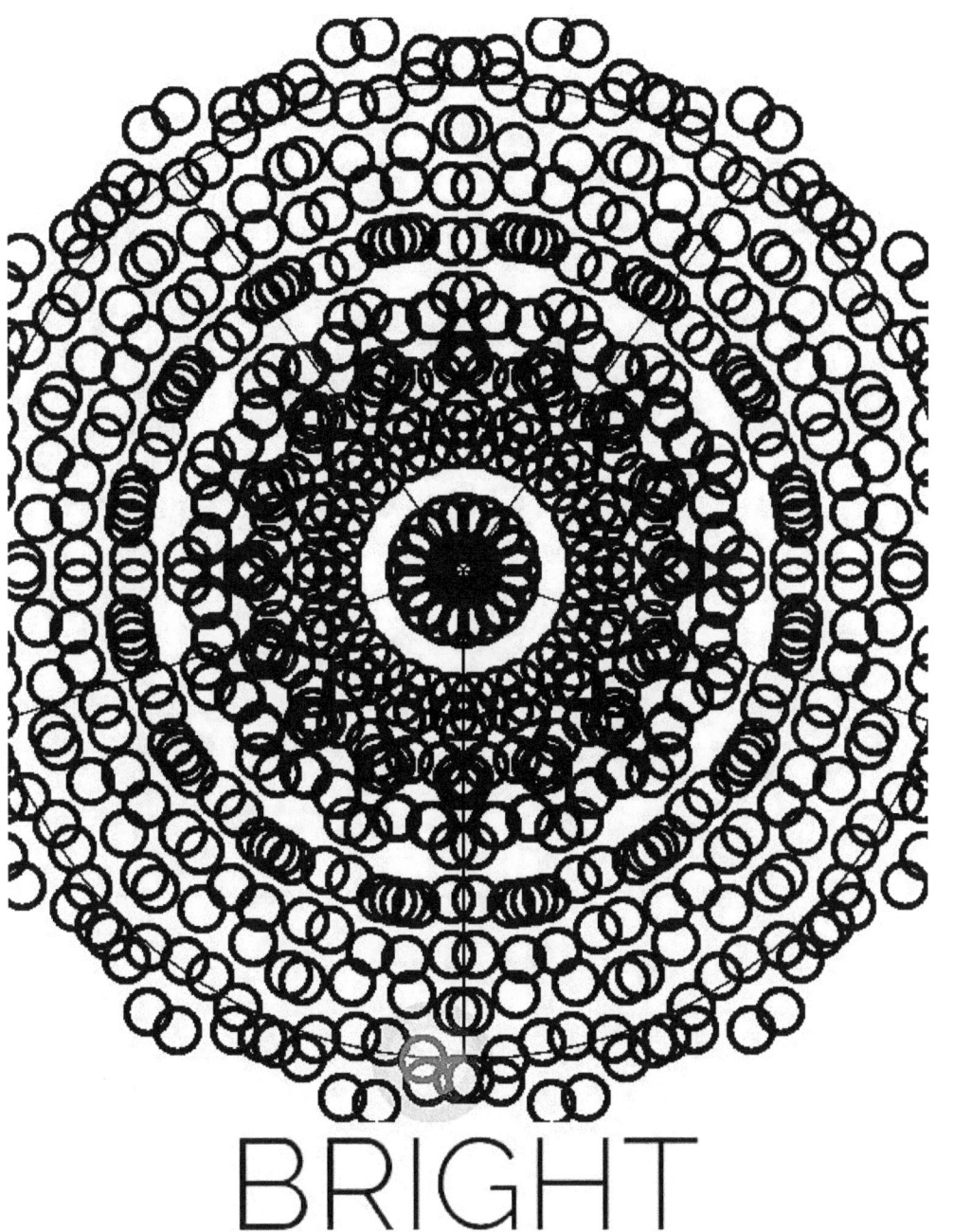

FIND YOUR FLOW

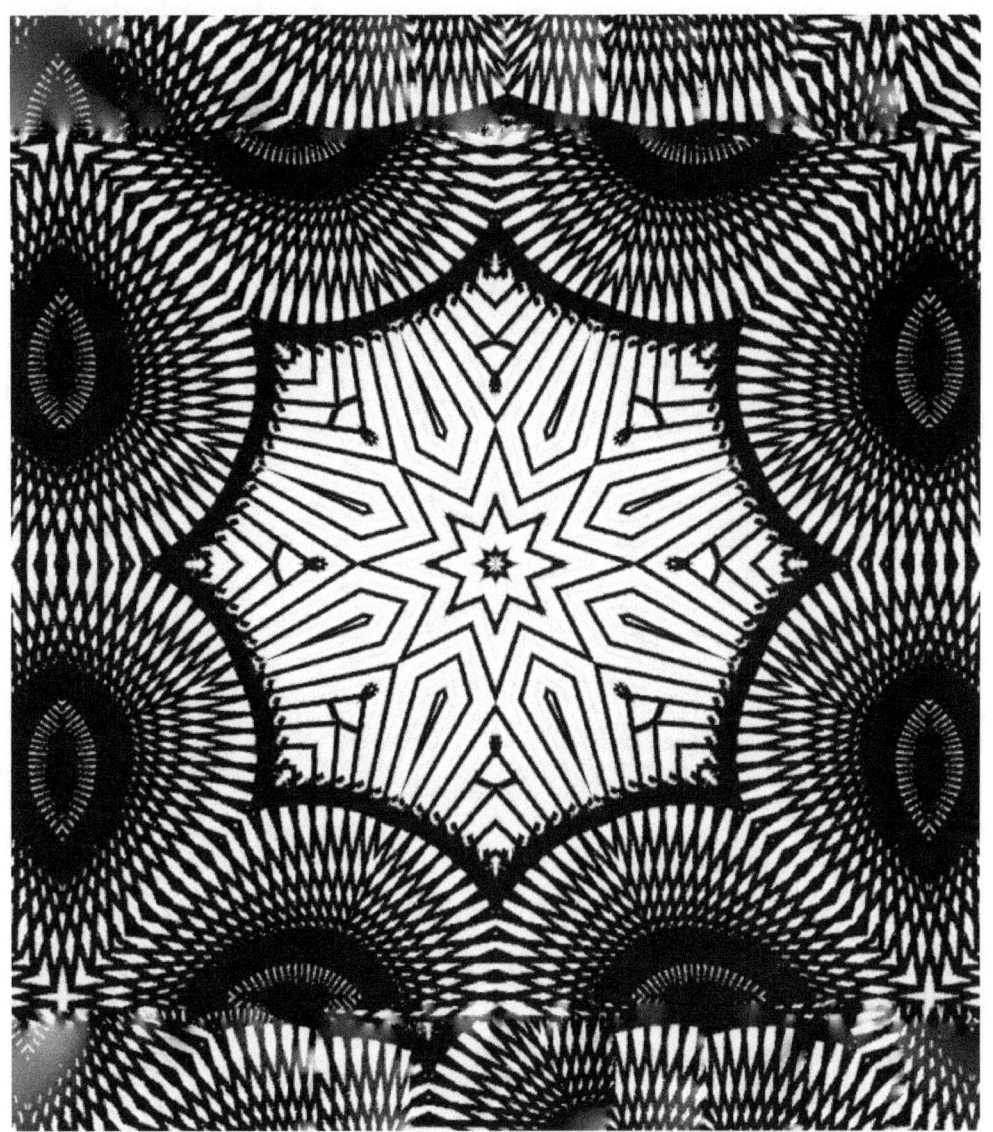

FIND YOUR GLOW

FEEL LIFE

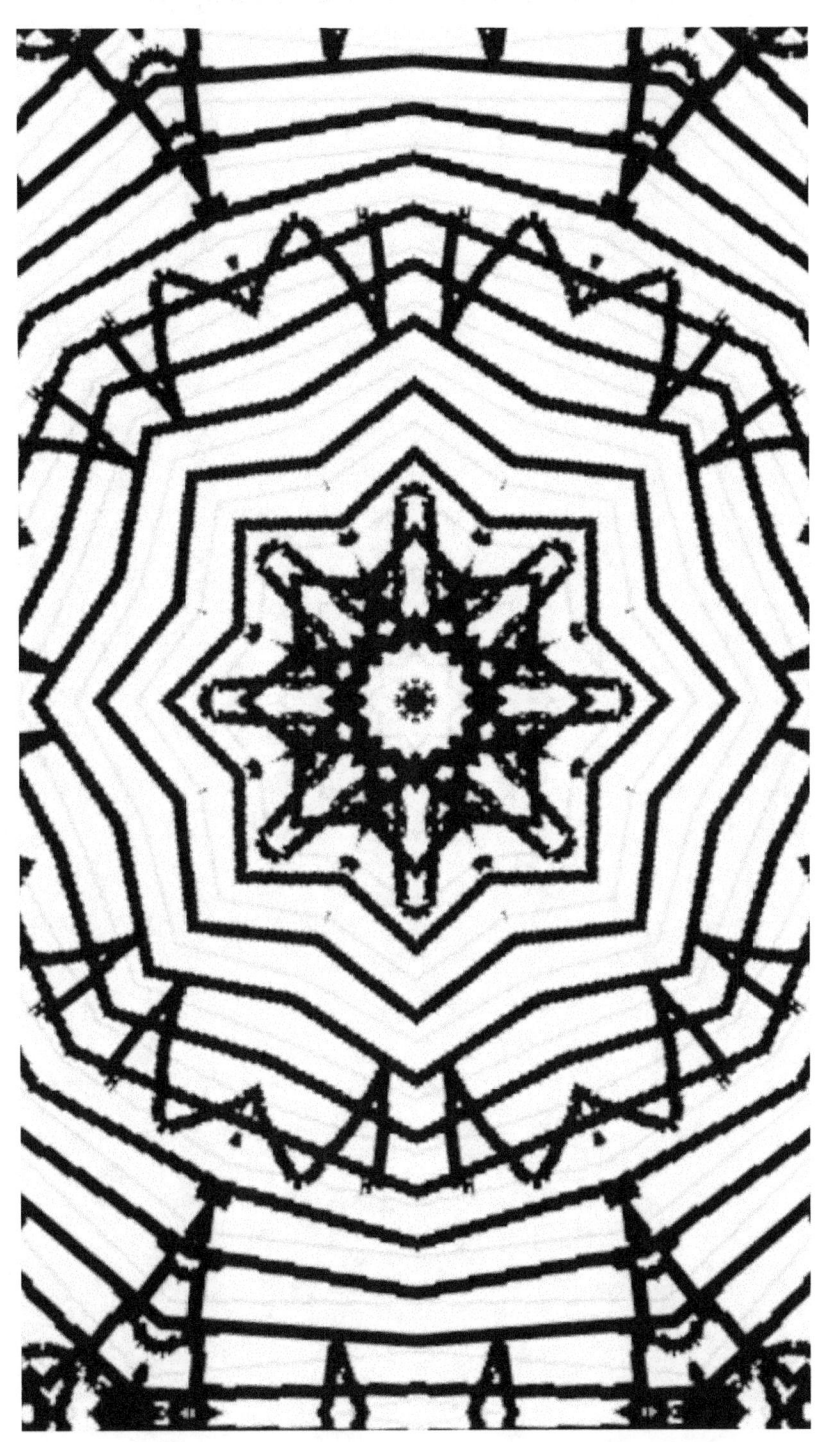

EACH BREATH

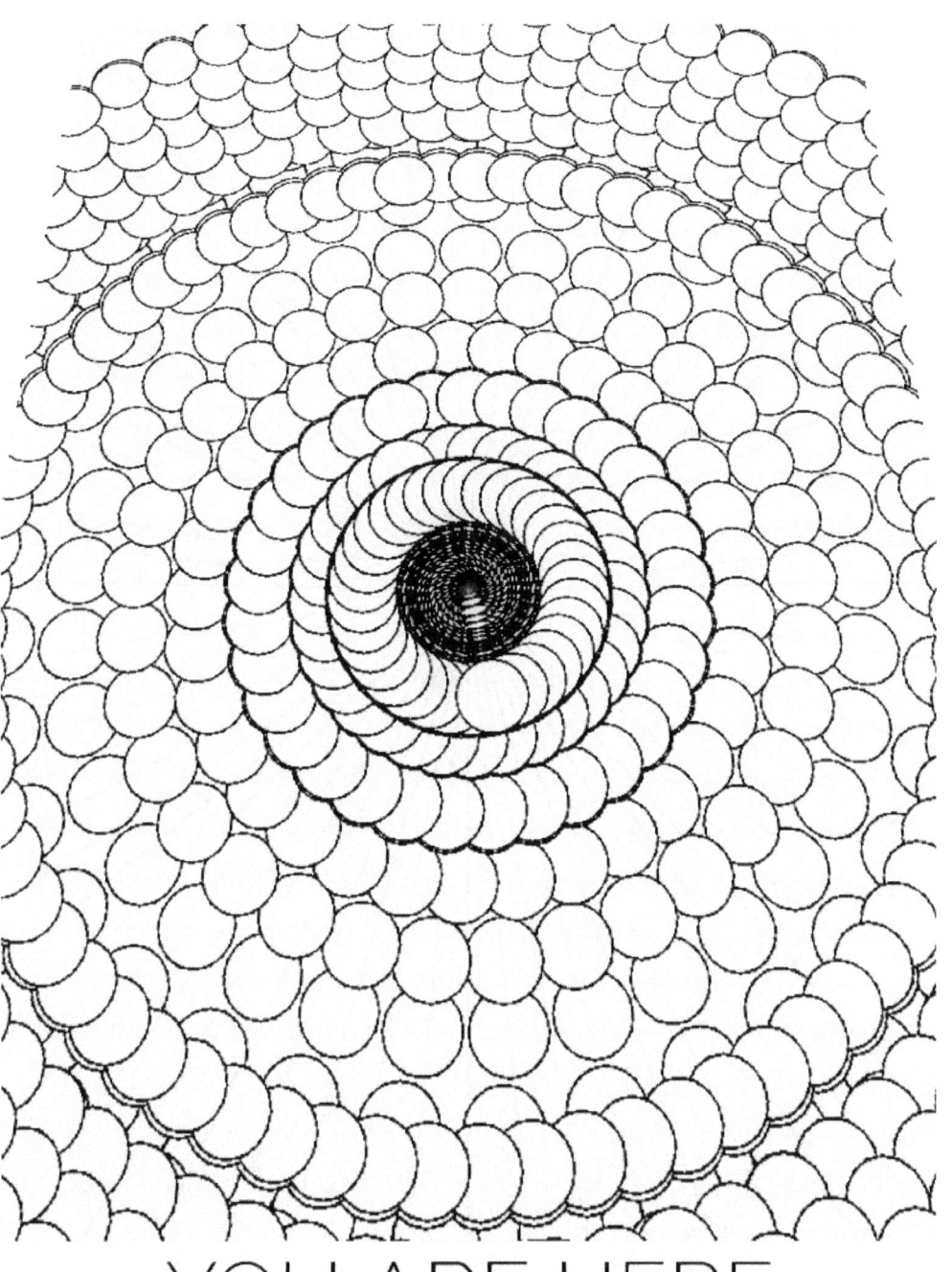

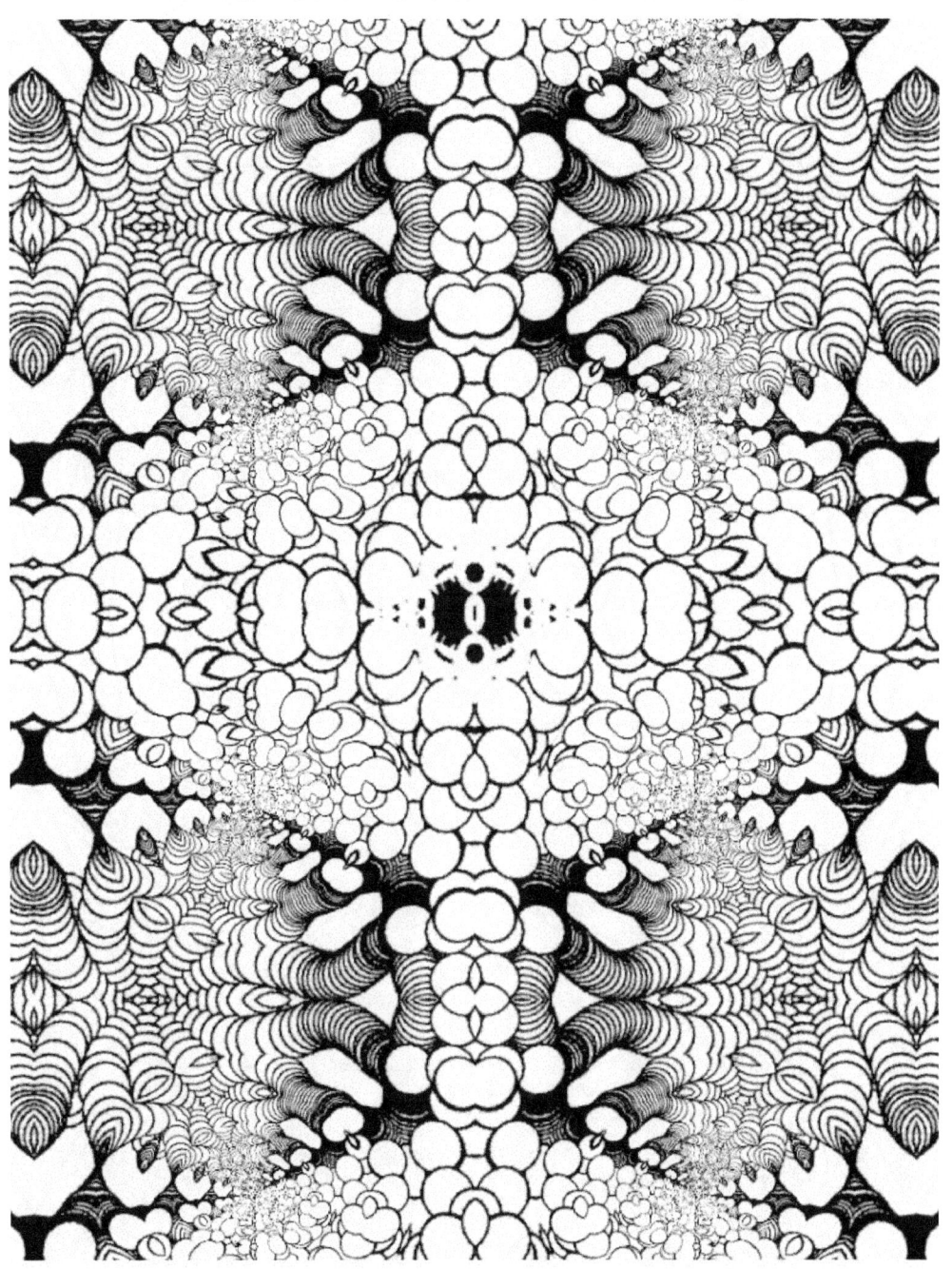

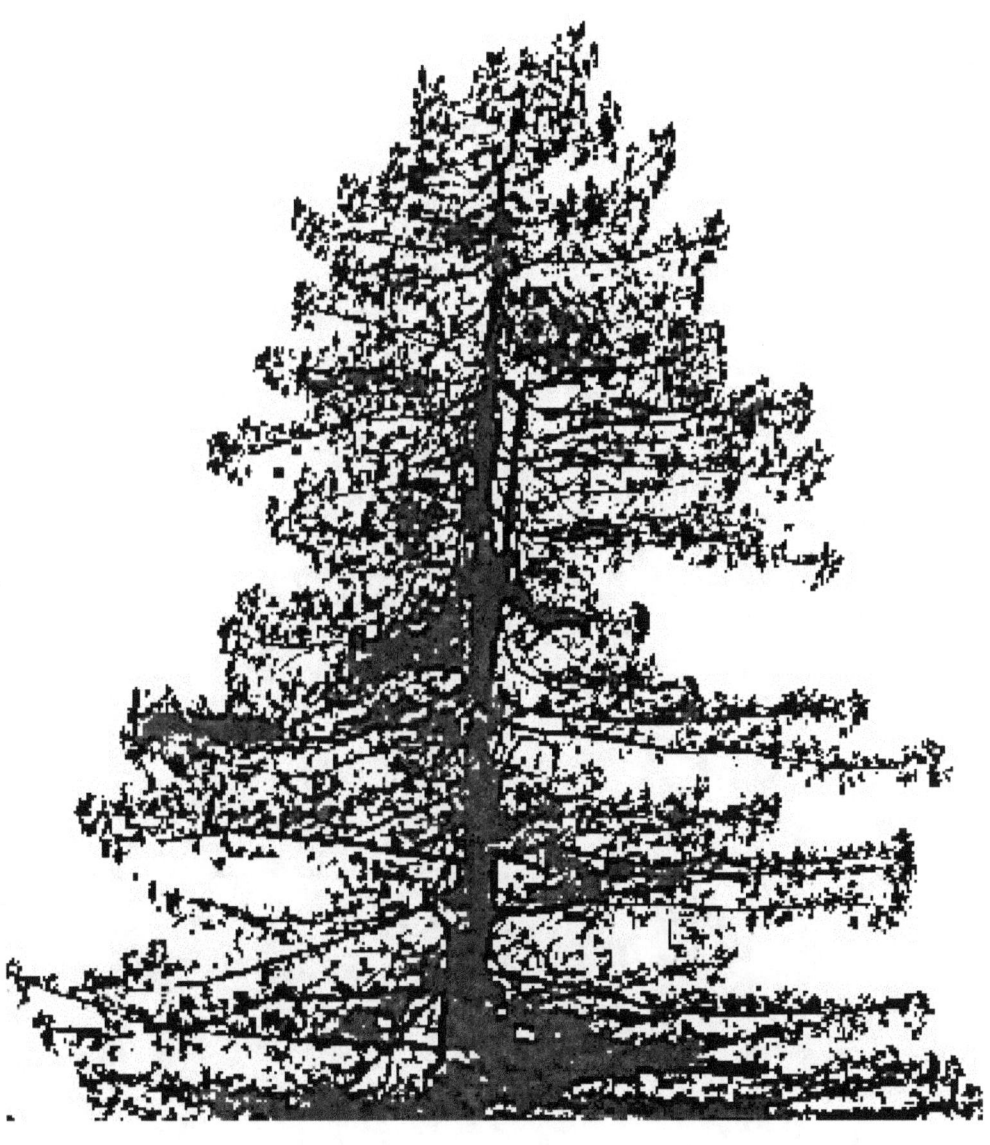

YOU CAN DO ANYTHING

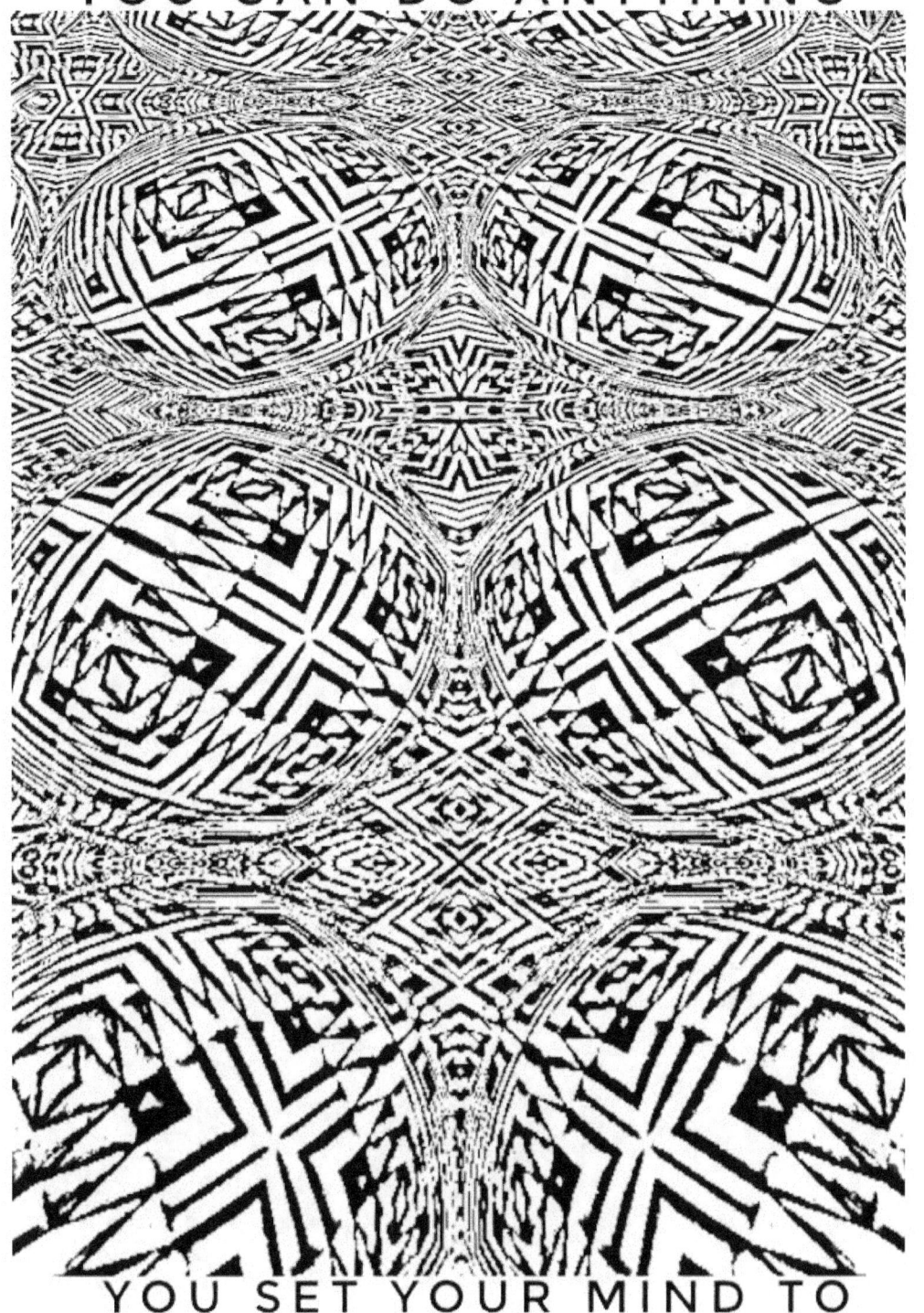

YOU SET YOUR MIND TO

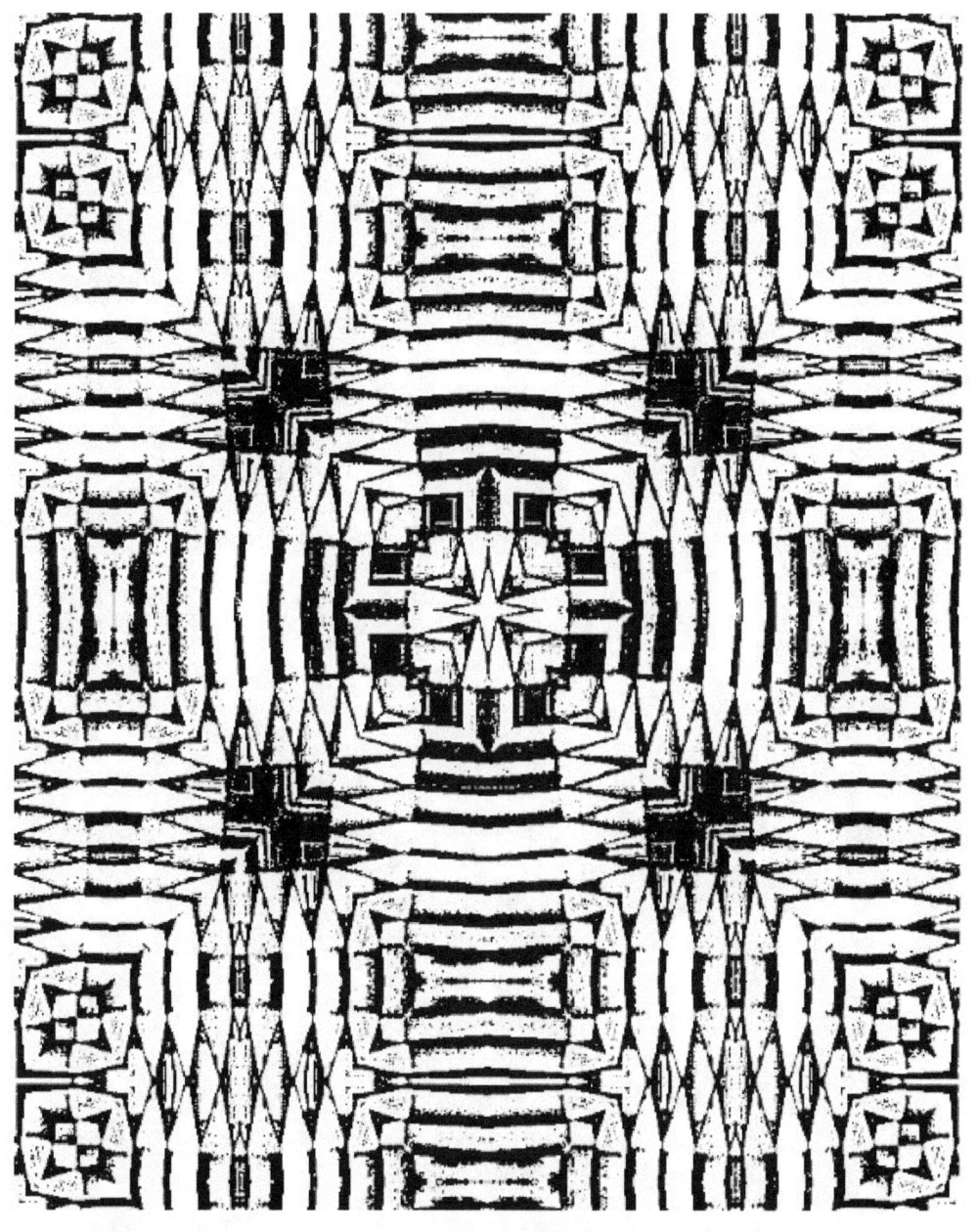

BUILD A BETTER YOU

JUST BE

YOUR POWERFUL

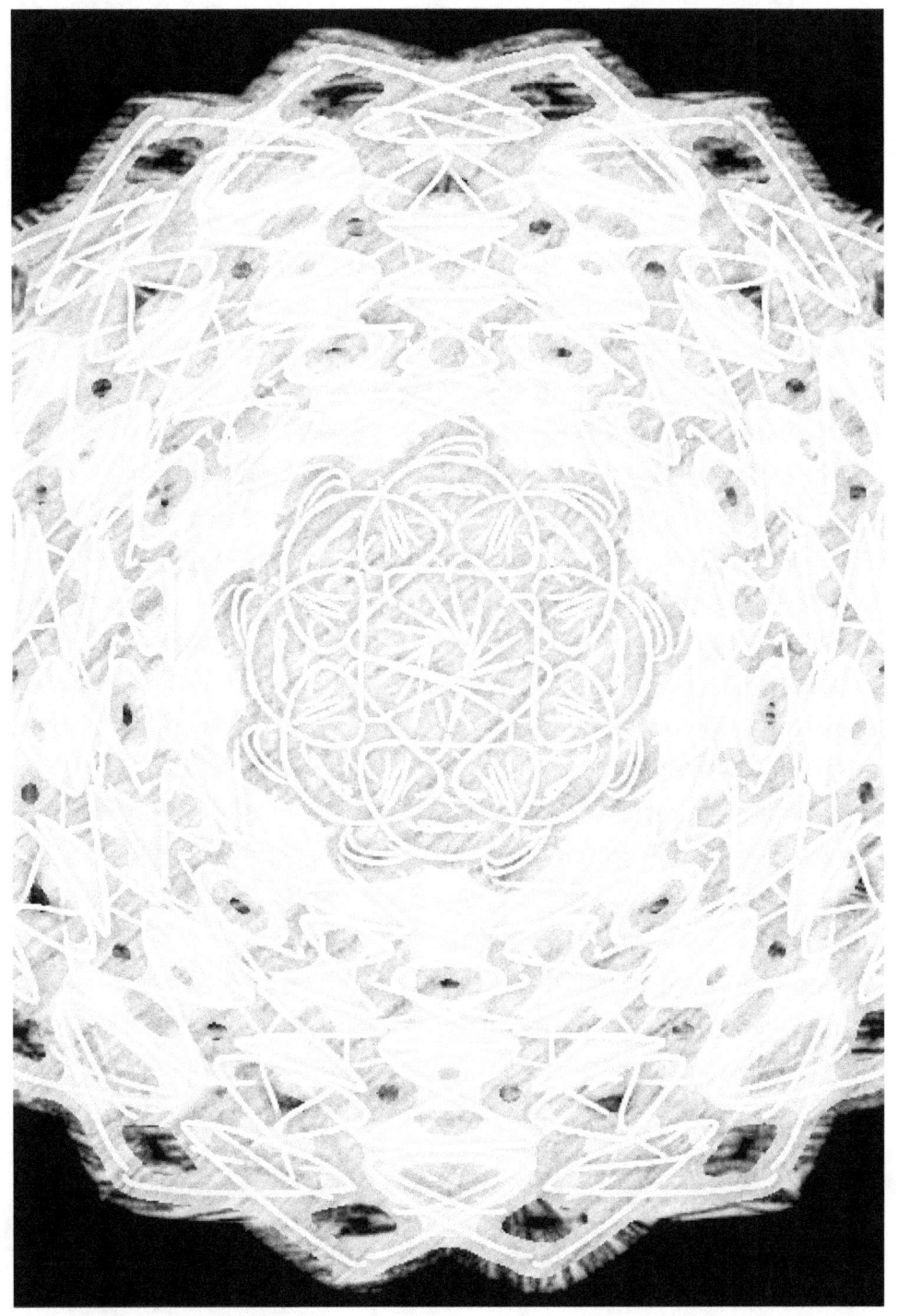

BEYOND IMAGINATION

www.ingramcontent.com/pod-product-compliance
Lightning Source LLC
Chambersburg PA
CBHW051531240526
45471CB00019B/712